D0431893

The Craft
COCKTAIL PARTY

DELICIOUS DRINKS FOR EVERY OCCASION

The Craft COCKTAIL PARTY

DELICIOUS DRINKS FOR EVERY OCCASION

Julie Reiner

WITH KAITLYN GOALEN

Photographs by Daniel Krieger

GRAND CENTRAL
Life & Style
NEW YORK • BOSTON

Grand Central Life & Style
Hachette Book Group
1290 Avenue of the Americas
New York, NY 10104

www.GrandCentralLifeandStyle.com

Printed in the United States of America

Q-MA

First Edition: May 2015
10 9 8 7 6 5 4 3 2 1

Grand Central Life & Style is an imprint of Grand Central
Publishing. The Grand Central Life & Style name and
logo are trademarks of Hachette Book Group, Inc.

The Hachette Speakers Bureau provides a wide range of
authors for speaking events. To find out more, go to www
.HachetteSpeakersBureau.com or call (866) 376-6591.

The publisher is not responsible for websites (or their content) that
are not owned by the publisher.

Library of Congress Cataloging-in-Publication Data
Reiner, Julie.
    The craft cocktail party : amazing drinks for every occasion / Julie
Reiner with Kaitlyn Goalen ; photographs by Daniel Krieger. —
First edition.
        pages cm
    Includes index.
    ISBN 978-1-4555-8159-7 (hardcover) —
ISBN 978-1-4555-8160-3 (ebook)   1. Cocktails.   I. Goalen,
Kaitlyn.   II. Title.
    TX951.R435 2015
    641.87'4—dc23
                                                2014049853

6051 0673 07/15

For my Mom,

WHO TAUGHT ME ABOUT
THE ART OF HOSPITALITY AND
THE SIMPLE JOYS OF LIFE.

CONTENTS

FOREWORD
A Look Behind the Curtain

BY DALE DEGROFF

I HAD A FUN BUSINESS FOR A MINUTE in New York City in the 1990s: the Cocktail Safari, a culinary and cocktail walking tour of four different spots—at each we would taste three small cocktails matched with small bites. I nosed around bars and restaurants in different neighborhoods searching out innovative menus with small bites and cocktails. They were not so easy to find in the mid-1990s, but there are always creative people and I found them. I was visiting a small hotel bar called C3 Lounge on Washington Square Park when I encountered one of those creative people. Her name was Julie Reiner.

Julie had a quick smile, a snappy shaking style, and served some very tasty drinks. I can't remember if our safari got there in time to enjoy her creations, but I certainly did, and I made sure that anyone I spoke to from the industry and press did as well. It seems we all did too good of a job spreading the word, because when Julie ended up with a small notice in the *New York Times*, the chef decided that if anyone in that operation was going to get some press it should be him, and he thought Julie was going to open her own place and steal the clientele, so he had her fired.

The last thirty years have seen a sea change in the culinary world. Barriers dissolved as chefs viewed cuisine not as representative of different culinary cultures, but as fair game for crafting personal styles and creative growth. Techniques from one culture were applied to ingredients and recipes from another. Ethnic and regional cuisines expanded beyond their borders. Nouvelle, California, Fusion, and Locavore cuisines emerged, and diners were treated to a whole new world of flavor.

The flavor evolution did not stop with the kitchen, however. The first fourteen years of the new millennium have transformed the American cocktail. A willing public, in love with big flavor and ready to experiment, found the mundane offerings at the traditional bars unsatisfactory. Bartending as a respected profession had disappeared during the Depression years, and without skilled professionals, the drinks business post-Prohibition was dumbed down. Skills were replaced with shortcuts, like artificial mixers and artificially flavored spirits. Now that is all changed.

The new millennium set the stage for a nascent craft cocktail movement, and Julie was right there at the outset. Techniques and ingredients found only in the chef's domain became the techniques and ingredients of the new "culinary cocktails." Julie spent those years developing and perfecting her special culinary approach to the bar, using fresh ingredients.

This is a special time for the bar industry worldwide, and there are a group of dedicated professionals who have moved the marker forward in this industry. Julie Reiner is one of those people.

Julie Reiner is the force behind two of the most iconic saloons in New York City: Flatiron Lounge, an oasis for discerning cocktailians in search of authentic craft cocktails in classic deco surroundings, opened in 2003. And Clover Club, on Smith Street in Brooklyn, pays homage to pre-Prohibition bar culture, a culture that has long been the benchmark for American bars around the world. Julie is also a partner in another beloved New York landmark—the Pegu Club—which she opened in 2005 with Audrey Saunders.

Great bars reflect the passion, knowledge, and presence of the proprietor, and they don't happen overnight; they happen because someone shows up and runs the joint. Julie has the work ethic reminiscent of that bygone era. She shows up and she runs the joint!

Her detailing is fine: You won't find a capsized lemon or orange peel floating in one of her cocktails. Julie's classic cocktails are authentic, and she is an artist with fresh fruit–based cocktails. Julie's back bar workbench has much in common with a restaurant garde-manger station with herbs and veggies, berries and exotic fruits, spices and house flavored syrups.

Julie and Audrey Saunders, her partner at Pegu Club, have created a workshop for excellence in craft bartending unmatched in our industry. Her three bars have turned out craft bartenders at a remarkable rate, many of whom have gone on to establish some of the best craft bar programs in the country, such as Mayahuel, PDT, Sweetwater Social, Pouring Ribbons, Dram, Victor Tangos in Dallas, and many others around the country.

The Craft Cocktail Party opens this culinary side of the drinks world to the reader in clear and simple prose, along with easy-to-follow recipes. These recipes will please everyone from the cocktail geek to the casual drinker. Julie presents the material in cookbook fashion with step-by-step instructions.

The lighthearted, celebratory ambiance that makes a trip to one of Julie's great saloons special informs the style of this book. Julie is serious about ingredients and quality, exacting in measurements. But she constantly reminds the reader to just have some fun with the recipes and their cocktails. She advises: Use regular household kitchen tools when possible. There's no need to spend a fortune to buy a serious professional set of tools. Substitute your favorite ingredients. *Play, invent, this is your own crib…get down and have a party!*

INTRODUCTION

The Bar Is Open...

CRAFT COCKTAILS—defined by proper technique and quality ingredients—were once accused of being just a trend that would fade after a few years, but I think it's clear that they are here to stay. There are so many amazing bartenders working hard to innovate the way we imbibe. It is an incredibly exciting time to go out for a drink.

While things have advanced behind the bar, cocktails have been slower to catch on at home. Many people have come to think of cocktails as being shrouded in mystery. The process of making them can seem overwhelming, what with all the specific tools and unfamiliar types of alcohol. Additionally, there is a certain amount of cultlike intensity that pervades the industry as a whole and that has, I believe, scared away first-timers from making their own drinks. My hope is that this book can help break through that layer of fog and demystify the cocktail for anyone.

After all, the drink itself is only half the puzzle. The reason I went into bartending in the first place, and what keeps me in the business, is something much larger than what's in the glass: Cocktails bring us together and help us celebrate.

My years behind the bar have only crystallized this truth for me. Night after night, I watch people meet for drinks to mark an occasion: a new job, an anniversary, a holiday, the arrival of a new season, or even just catching up with an old friend. Cocktails are tools of commemoration. We clink glasses to signify a moment worth remembering and to make ourselves feel good while we do it.

❧

I now realize that I was a host long before I tasted my first cocktail.

My mom and dad love entertaining. My earliest memories are of housefuls of people, dancing, great food, and the fancy "grown-up drinks" that seemed to facilitate the flow of laughter in the room. When I was a kid growing up in Hawaii, it was my job to pass hors d'oeuvres at my parents' cocktail parties while my mom would dole out drinks to our guests. I loved it; being a part of their festive occasions in any capacity made me feel

Blackberry Collins (page 179)

like I was sharing in the good time. I didn't know it then, but that act of welcoming someone into one's home with a glass of something refreshing and delicious made a permanent impression on me. My early juice-based mocktail experiments were always met with smiles, and I fell in love with the experience of the cocktail party. I was in awe of my parents and their ability to entertain large numbers of people with such ease and enjoyment. I would fight to stay awake past my bedtime so as not to miss a minute.

There are many things I love about being from Hawaii, and one of them is that really fresh ingredients are the norm. My childhood coincided with a dark era in cocktail history when drinks came in neon colors and were mixed with juices from concentrates. Luckily, such shortcuts never gained much traction on our island, where ripe, sweet pineapples, oversize guava, and bright citrus were available year-round. I fell in love with these fresh ingredients, and when I came of age, they became a part of my cocktail-making arsenal. As a result, I had high standards for what constituted a delicious drink from the very beginning.

I moved to San Francisco after college, and after a few attempts at finding a "real" job, I found myself cocktail waitressing and learning the basics of the hospitality industry. But my eureka moment didn't come until I started hanging out at the Red Room on Sutter Street. It was located near Union Square, just around the corner from my apartment, and I had watched the entire construction process, amazed at what the owners had done with the place. It was smart, sexy, and innovative, and was designed to provide a much-needed break from the grind of work and life stresses. The Red Room helped me begin to understand the art of creating an environment that facilitates an escape.

The Red Room had great design and music, and the bar stocked only the freshest ingredients, but the biggest revelation was the bartenders: They were all women, and they were the best in town. This was the first place I had been that shattered the boys' club behind the bar and also raised the stakes for artisanal bartending. These women put out a high volume of well-crafted drinks with great service. They managed to create a party during every shift, with each night's energy eclipsing that of the night before. I looked at their bar with the same admiration that I had for my parents' cocktail parties, and it clicked: This was what I was supposed to do.

Since I had no bartending experience, I convinced one of the bartenders to let me slip behind the bar for a few minutes here and there to "stage" with her. I learned the ropes of the Red Room's ahead-of-the-curve cocktail program quickly. They were using fresh juices, a few homemade syrups, and premium liquors to execute their classically focused menu.

Three years later, after I had bartended around the Bay Area, I moved to New York City and started hunting for a job. I went from bar to bar and was shocked: I saw cans of juice, bottles of sugary soda, and week-old garnishes. I wondered how New Yorkers, who were notorious for demanding the best of everything, could accept such mediocrity when it came to drinks. When I took a job running the bar at C3 in the Washington Square Hotel, I created a program based on the foundation I'd built in Hawaii and at the Red Room—focusing on fresh fruit as cocktail ingredients—and people responded, in droves.

It wasn't until New York that I got my first dose of real seasons. The winters I'd experienced in Hawaii and San Francisco couldn't compare with the temperature drop on the East Coast. The seasons became my muses behind the bar: I made apple infusions in the fall, relied on hot toddies to keep my guests warm in the winter, celebrated spring with bright and light aperitifs, and returned to my roots in the summer, making drinks with an emphasis on whatever was fresh and at its peak at the market.

My two bars, Flatiron Lounge in Manhattan and Clover Club in Brooklyn, still adhere to this basic philosophy, offering a blend of smartly executed classics and seasonally driven contemporary creations. Flatiron Lounge, which opened in 2003, is my homage to the glitz and glamour of old-school New York. The centerpiece of the room, a twenty-foot bar, has a long history: It was originally in an illegal bar in Brooklyn during Prohibition, then it moved to the Ballroom, a Rat Pack hangout. In the eighties, it lived at Catch a Rising Star. I love that Flatiron Lounge is now a part of this city's incredible nightlife lineage.

Clover Club opened a few years later and takes inspiration from a very specific period in cocktail history: pre-Prohibition. By serving drinks from the era in which the cocktail was born, our bar serves as an abbreviated timeline, with a menu that shows the evolution of cocktails.

Since I first arrived in New York, a lot has changed in cocktail culture, and mostly for the better. The cans of juice and crappy garnishes are now endangered species, and many bartenders are sticklers for fresh ingredients. Craft cocktails were once a rarity, and now they are quickly becoming the norm. And this trend is no longer isolated in large metropolises; you can drink well in almost every city in the country.

Just like good food, cocktails are best when shared—whether at your favorite neighborhood bar, at a four-star restaurant, or at home on a Tuesday night. The truth is that a good drink is never more than five minutes away; cocktails are incredibly easy to make at home, provided you have a few basic spirits on hand, some fresh juice, and ice. There's a reason why some of the most classic drinks are the simplest.

This book wasn't written for the cocktail aficionado (although I think there are plenty of recipes in here that a booze geek could love). Rather, it is meant for those who like to gather around the table with family and friends to celebrate. Some of these recipes are proven favorites from my bars, adapted for the home; others are entirely new creations. I've organized the recipes by season and occasion, since those are generally the deciding factors when choosing what to drink at home. Within each chapter, though, there are also plenty of techniques that will find year-round use in your kitchen, including recipes for easy syrups and infusions. From the Fourth of July through New Year's and on to Mardi Gras, you'll always find a reason to raise a glass with friends. I hope this book will inspire your next memory-making party.

GETTING STARTED

Tools and Techniques

THIS BOOK IS *NOT* A COMPREHENSIVE GUIDE TO BARTENDING. It is specifically tailored to making drinks at home, with an eye toward entertaining. Rules bend a little more easily at home than behind a professional bar, so feel free to take certain liberties. If you don't have a muddler, use a wooden spoon; if you don't have a specific brand of gin, use what you *do* have. All that being said, having the correct equipment and basic technique will improve the cocktails you make, so here are some very general guidelines that are worth perusing before you set out on your boozy adventure.

TOOLS

To make the recipes in this book, you'll need a few things. Just like with cooking tools, some things are more essential than others, but most of the equipment needed to build your bar is fairly affordable and easy to find, which makes it worth the investment.

MEASURING COCKTAILS

Ounces are the standard unit of measure for making single-serving cocktails. Behind the bar we use two-sided vessels called jiggers, which come in the most commonly used volumes. For home use, I recommend the 1-and-2-ounce jigger from Cocktail Kingdom, which has demarcations for all the major measurements you'll need. Another alternative is the Oxo Mini Angled Measuring Cup, which measures up to 2 ounces. When you measure, take care to fill your jigger or

measuring cup all the way to the widest point to make sure you're getting the right volume in your drink.

SHAKING AND STIRRING

The next thing you'll need is a shaker. This instrument has two purposes: simultaneously blending together the various ingredients of your drink and chilling the mixture through the presence of ice. It also introduces air into the drink, which changes the texture and consistency. There are several types of shakers out there; choose the one that works best for you.

Boston shaker (I): Consists of a pint glass and a 28-ounce metal mixing tin that goes over the glass to create a seal. The pint glass can double as a mixing glass for stirred drinks. Use this in conjunction with a Hawthorne strainer.

Tin-on-tin shaker (2): Consists of a short 18-ounce metal tin and a tall 28-ounce metal mixing tin that fit together to create a seal. This style of shaker is the bartender's choice, as it is lighter than the Boston shaker and can't be broken. Use this in conjunction with a Hawthorne strainer.

Cobbler shaker (3): Consists of a metal tin, a top with a built-in strainer, and a twist-off cap. Cobbler shakers are fine for home use, but not quite as versatile as Boston shakers. It is also very easy to lose the cap…at least in my house!

Certain drinks, specifically those made with only spirituous ingredients (such as an Old Fashioned or a Manhattan), should not be made in a shaker. Instead, we mix them by gently stirring them, which produces a silkier texture. To make a stirred drink, you'll need a mixing glass and a bar spoon.

Mixing glass (4): A large glass with a spout. They range in size from 15 to 40 ounces. Use this in conjunction with a julep strainer.

Bar spoon (5): A spoon with an elongated handle to make stirring the contents of your cocktail easier. The volume of a bar spoon is approximately 1 teaspoon.

Generally we strain cocktails from our shaker or mixing glass into our drinking glass to keep the shaking ice and solids (such as fruit or herbs) out of the finished drink. To do this, we can use a few different kinds of strainers.

Hawthorne strainer (6): A strainer with a metal coil that fits snugly inside the metal tin, keeping the ice inside when you strain your cocktail. It is used in conjunction with the Boston or tin-on-tin shaker. This is the most versatile strainer, as it will also fit inside your mixing glass.

Julep strainer (7): A strainer with small holes that keep ice out of the drink, used to strain stirred drinks from a mixing glass.

Fine-mesh sieve (8): A cone-shaped strainer lined with mesh, used to strain solids out of a cocktail. It is used in conjunction with a Hawthorne strainer for a process called double straining.

16 12 11 14 10

GLASSWARE

So you've mixed up a drink and are ready to strain it into a glass and enjoy the fruit of your labor. Which glass do you use? Here's where you have options. While certain cocktails are married to certain types of glasses (like the Old Fashioned, which should be served in—you guessed it—an Old Fashioned glass), others are more flexible. I've included my suggestion for which type of glass you should use with every recipe, but you shouldn't feel obligated to go out and blow your budget on specialty crystal.

As you start to make cocktails with more frequency, it's likely that you'll slowly amass your own collection of specific glassware. Personally, I love to buy my glasses and punch bowls at antique stores, because each piece has its own personality. But I also keep a stash of basic, durable glasses that I pull out when entertaining friends. They are less likely to break and easy to replace if they do.

Whenever possible, chill your glassware before you pour a drink into it. This will preserve all the hard work you did with your shaker or bar spoon to get the drink cold in the first place. To chill your glass you can either store it in the freezer or fill it with ice and water for a few minutes before you mix your drink.

Here are the most frequently used glasses behind the cocktail bar:

Champagne Flute (9): A narrow, stemmed glass used for cocktails topped with sparkling wine, such as the French 75.

Collins (10): Slightly thinner and taller than the highball, the Collins glass generally holds 12 to 14 ounces. It's used for drinks topped with soda…like the Tom Collins.

Coupe (11): Also called a "cocktail glass," this stemmed, saucer-shaped glass is best used

for drinks served without ice (up) that include citrus, like the Daiquiri. A proper coupe should hold approximately 6 ounces.

Highball (12): A tall glass that generally holds 10 to 12 ounces and is used for long drinks; suitable for any highball cocktail with soda or a classic fizz served without ice.

Hurricane (13): An exotic 15-ounce glass used for tropical drinks. Named after its hurricane-lamp shape.

Julep (14): The traditional silver or pewter stemless cup used to serve the mint julep.

Martini (15): Also called a "cocktail glass," this V-shaped stemmed glass is best used for drinks without ice, ranging from 6 to 8 ounces.

Nick and Nora (16): A retro-style stemmed glass used for stirred cocktails like the Martini and Manhattan. It should hold 4 to 5 ounces.

Rocks or Old Fashioned (17): A short, sturdy stemless glass that usually holds 10 to 12 ounces; great for spirits and cocktails served over ice.

Wine goblet (18): A large, balloon-shaped wineglass, ideal for fancy cocktails such as the Blush Baby (page 22).

TECHNIQUE

At its core, the process of preparing a cocktail is really simple. There are two main goals: combining ingredients and chilling them. The ingredients in the cocktail recipe determine the technique you should use. (For more information, see "Dilution and Chilling" sidebar on page 28.)

Shaking: This is the method to use when working with thick or pulpy ingredients, such as citrus, milk, and eggs. Combine the desired ingredients in the bottom of a shaker and add ice. Seal the shaker and shake it quickly back and forth with some force until the outside begins to frost, about 20 to 25 seconds.

Stirring: This technique is primarily used for cocktails with exclusively alcoholic ingredients, such as the Gin Blossom (page 96). By stirring the drink, you are chilling it without aerating, which results in a smoother cocktail. Start by adding your ingredients to your mixing glass. Add ice and stir with a bar spoon for 20 to 25 seconds.

Rolling: This technique is somewhere in between shaking and stirring. We use it for drinks that require more agitation than a stirred cocktail but shouldn't, for whatever reason, be fully shaken. The Bloody Mary is a great example: Shaking aerates the tomato juice too much, while stirring doesn't fully disperse the thicker ingredients. First, combine your ingredients in the glass that you will serve the drink in and add ice. Pour the contents of the glass into your large mixing tin, then pour the contents back and forth between your large tin and your small tin. Do this five times and then pour the contents, including the ice, into the original glass and serve.

JUICING

Fresh-squeezed juice is imperative to a well-made cocktail. Resist the urge to buy bottled "fresh" juice; buy whole citrus instead, juicing it just before you're ready to make your drink. For basic juicing at home, the hand juicer is your best option. This tool is affordable and takes up very little counter space. If you throw

a lot of large parties, you may want to invest in an electric juicer that will make the job quick and easy. Here are some tips for becoming a juice ninja:

Warm it up. As my friend and bar professional Tony Abou-Ganim says, "Cold fruit is stingy fruit." By allowing your citrus to come to room temperature before you juice it, you'll improve your yield significantly. I don't always remember to take my lemons and limes out of the refrigerator ahead of time, so I'll give them a quick soak in warm water (for about 15 minutes) to speed up the process.

Grow a thin skin. When choosing fruit for juicing, look for heavier fruit with the thinnest skin. The more flesh, the more juice.

Roll with it. Before cutting your fruit in half, roll it on the counter under your palm. This will break the cells in the fruit and help to release the juice.

Go pulp free. Always strain your citrus juice through a fine-mesh sieve to remove the pulp before adding it to your cocktail. Your drinks will be pulp free and your glassware will be easier to clean.

Same-day service. Try to prepare your juice as close to your party as you can, no more than 8 hours ahead of time.

Leftovers. Lemon and lime juice oxidizes quickly, causing it to become bitter, so don't save any leftovers. Orange and grapefruit juice, on the other hand, will keep in your refrigerator for 2 to 3 days after juicing.

Garnishes

My obsession with garnishes is sort of an inside joke among the bartenders who work with me. I'm known for creating elaborate spears, long loop twists, and miniature floral arrangements to adorn every cocktail. Why? You drink a cocktail with your eyes before you drink it with your mouth: Garnishes elevate the cocktail to an even more celebratory status. The garnishes for the recipes in this book are worth preparing if you have time; certainly they create a more festive vibe if you are entertaining. But at the end of the day, they're optional. If you want to make one of these recipes but don't have the garnish ingredients on hand, I won't fault you for leaving your cocktail naked.

CITRUS TWIST

There is a caveat to the "optional" element of garnishing: the citrus twist. This garnish is actually essential to the flavor and composition of the drink. Citrus twists are a fixture in cocktail recipes because the essential oils in citrus peels act as ingredients in their own right. Citrus twists are also different from other garnishes in that they need to be "activated" before they're added to a drink. To do so, hold the twist lengthwise between the thumb and forefinger of each hand. Twist over the glass with the peel facing toward the surface of the cocktail. This will release the essential oils onto the drink. Then rub the peel's skin around the rim of the glass before dropping it into the drink, skin side up.

You can cut citrus twists with a paring knife or a vegetable peeler, and can store them in a glass with a wet paper towel for up to 5 hours.

For a more decorative version, you can create a long spiral citrus twist. Because it has less surface area and therefore less oil, it won't be as flavorful as a regular twist, so I wouldn't recommend it in drinks like the Old Fashioned or Martini, where that oil is crucial to the composition of the drink. Oxo makes a few different peelers to create both spiral twists and long twists. These peelers have a long life before they become dull and need to be replaced. A channel knife can also be used to cut the long spiral twists recommended for many cocktails in this book.

Simple Syrup

This bar staple is a must for making balanced cocktails. Very plainly, we use simple syrup to introduce sugar to a cocktail in a form that is already dissolved. The basic (simple) ratio is equal parts granulated sugar and water. Consider it a guiding light to the syrup recipes you'll find in this book; all of them build on this basic combination. I make simple syrup in a batch of one cup sugar to one cup water at home. It keeps in the refrigerator for up to a month, but you'll likely go through a batch in way less time.

If you're not planning on making alcohol-free drinks, you can also fortify your syrups by adding 1 ounce vodka for every 10 ounces syrup. This will help preserve the syrup for an additional two to three weeks.

Throughout the book you'll find recipes for many different kinds of flavored syrups, which really enhance your cocktails.

Eggs

Many classic cocktails call for egg whites, which create a rich, creamy texture and a frothy cap.

Egg whites do not add flavor, so don't fear an eggy-tasting drink. You can also rest easy about salmonella: Just use the freshest eggs you can find, and rinse them thoroughly before cracking. The eggs that we have today are about twice the size of the eggs that were used when these drinks were first created, so use about half an egg white for the best results.

Ice

Ice is probably the most important ingredient when it comes to making drinks; it's also the most easily overlooked. If you plan to make cocktails for a large group (more than four people), you'll need an ice plan to make sure you don't run out of the stuff right in the middle of your Martinis. If you have a lot

of freezer space, you can make ice ahead of time. But if storage is limited, I'd recommend buying it.

For shaking and stirring ice, look for larger cubes. If you're making cobblers, juleps, or other crushed-ice cocktails, look for smaller, chippy ice.

You will generally need about 1½ to 2 pounds of ice for each guest. This number varies depending on the type of drinks you plan to make. For instance, if you're serving a punch, you won't need as much ice. Ditto if you're serving "up" drinks such as Daiquiris. But if you're making "long" drinks, such as Gin Fizzes, estimate a heavier allotment (2 pounds at least) for each person.

Ice, like anything else, is better when fresh. It absorbs the odors and flavors of the freezer really effectively, so it's best to use new ice, made as close to the date of your event as possible. If you're making ice ahead of time, be sure to store it in Ziploc freezer bags to keep it fresh.

YIELD

It's general practice to prepare cocktails in individual portions. Most of the recipes in this book are organized accordingly; all recipes make one serving unless otherwise specified. I have also included several recipes for larger groups, such as punches and party drinks; those yields are indicated in servings.

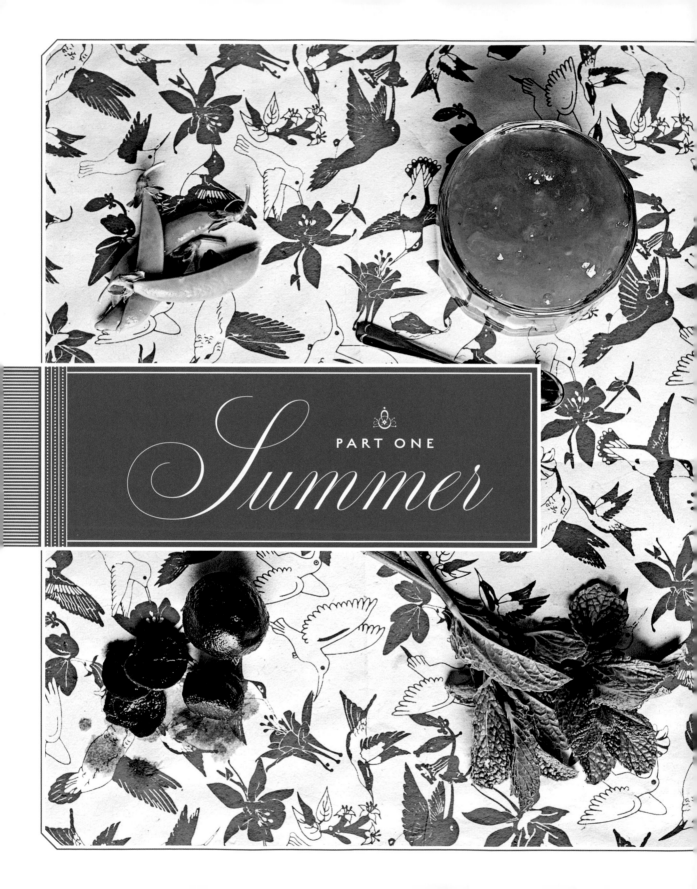

PART ONE

Summer

SUMMER IS THE TIME WHEN I KNOW I'M WORKING WITH A FULL TOOL KIT.

AT THE SEASON'S HEIGHT, when every stand at the farmers' market sags under the weight of pristine berries, plump tomatoes, and bunches of fragrant herbs, my bar starts to resemble a garden. I generally divide my market haul into two piles: one for muddling into drinks and one for making infusions and syrups. When certain fruits, like raspberries, are gently heated in sugar, the resulting syrup can be even more robust in flavor than the fruit itself.

Summer is also the time for the tropical drinks I grew up with. Nothing can transport me to a place of relaxation quicker than a giant swizzle glass filled to the brim with crushed ice and enough rum to make a pirate cry. Modern tropical cocktails and their close cousins, classic tiki drinks, are delightful conversation starters.

Some of my favorite summer recipes are the most ambitious ones in this book. Many cocktails in this part call for special syrups or infusions that make use of the season's fresh fruit. But don't be intimidated by the extra steps: I've included recipes for these prepared ingredients. Make the syrups or infusions at the beginning of the week; they keep wonderfully in the refrigerator, and you'll be able to mix up these recipes in a flash.

On holidays, I break out the "lazy bar." Nobody, myself included, wants to be chained to a shaker all day while the rest of the party is taking place around the grill or in the water. On these days, I batch—that is, I premix drinks in larger, group-size quantities. Sometimes it's a punch bowl, other times it's pitchers of Daiquiris. I'll set it out next to some glasses and an ice chest so my guests can help themselves and I get to enjoy the sunshine.

Sometimes, when I'm feeling *really* lazy, I don't even mix ahead. When we visit my in-laws in New Jersey for Labor Day, the first thing I do is set up a simple bar: bottles of vodka, gin, and rum; a few carafes of fresh juices; a beaker of simple syrup; and some garnishes. I'll make the first round of drinks to get everybody going, and then leave laminated copies of a few easy, delicious recipes out for the thirsty to help themselves while I'm in the pool.

1

Farmers' Market

Growing up in Hawaii, I was completely spoiled by fresh produce. My favorite fruits were in season essentially all year long. When I moved to New York that changed dramatically: Trying to eat a strawberry or a tomato in December became a depressing experience. As much as I sometimes miss the year-round access to ingredients that I had in Hawaii, the arrival of summer is so much more exciting to me in New York because I've spent the past nine months waiting for it. When I eat the season's first berries or peaches, it feels like a reunion with an old friend that I haven't seen in some time.

Many people don't automatically think of produce when making cocktails, but the truth is that fruits and vegetables are major cornerstones of any good bar.

At my bar Clover Club, we have devoted an entire section of the menu to drinks that are inspired by what's in season. In the summer, there are drinks with strawberries, blackberries, and raspberries, of course, but we also make use of fresh herbs and savory produce like tomatoes and corn. When the weather turns cooler, beets stain our cocktails, and in spring one of my bartenders makes an amazing cocktail with sugar snap peas! There is no limit to what you can do.

LA ROSA

You'd never think that tequila and amaro, the classic Italian digestif, would make sense together in a cocktail. Enter the strawberry, which somehow brings these strong spirits into harmony.

1 strawberry, hulled

½ ounce simple syrup

2 ounces blanco tequila (I recommend Cabeza)

1 ounce amaro (I recommend Ramazzotti)

¾ ounce lemon juice

1½ ounces sparkling rosé wine

Garnish / Spiral lemon twist

In the bottom of a shaker, muddle the strawberry in the simple syrup. Add the tequila, amaro, and lemon juice and shake with ice. Double-strain through a fine-mesh sieve into a Martini glass and top with the sparkling rosé. Garnish with the lemon twist.

MUDDLING

The simplest way to incorporate fresh fruit in a cocktail is through muddling. The main tool for the job, a muddler, looks a bit like an elongated pestle and comes in an array of sizes and materials. (I prefer muddlers made of wood.) In a pinch, a wooden kitchen spoon works just as well. To muddle, just drop your fruit into the bottom of your cocktail shaker and use your muddler to mash the fruit by pressing down in two or three firm pushes—you don't want to completely pulverize the fruit, merely bruise it enough that it releases its juices. Then you can add the rest of your ingredients. Just make sure to double-strain, which is bartender-speak for straining the cocktail through a Hawthorne strainer and a fine-mesh sieve held over the glass to catch the fruit's solids.

MARIA SIN SANGRE

Think of this drink as a Bloody Mary on the fly. Forget the
canned tomato juice; here, the freshness of summer's favorite fruit
is muddled directly into the drink.

---

6 cherry tomatoes

6 basil leaves

½ ounce simple syrup

2 ounces blanco tequila (I recommend El Tesoro)

½ ounce dry sherry (I recommend Williams & Humbert medium-dry)

½ ounce lemon juice

Pinch salt and pepper

Garnish / 1 cherry tomato and 1 basil leaf

In the bottom of a shaker, muddle the tomatoes and basil in the simple syrup. Add the
tequila, sherry, lemon juice, salt, and pepper and shake with ice until chilled. Double-
strain through a fine-mesh sieve into a coupe glass.

To create the garnish, pierce a small hole in the top of the tomato and insert the stem of
the basil leaf like a flag. Make a slit in the bottom of the tomato and perch the tomato on
the rim of the glass.

PRO TIP

*To make this drink in larger yields, pulse the
tomatoes and basil in a food processor 5 or 6
times, then strain through a fine-mesh sieve or
a piece of cheesecloth and discard the solids.*

SLOE & LOW

Sloe gin, an invention of the British, is infused with sloe berries.
To bring that flavor to the fore, this drink calls for both raspberries and
blackberries and is capped off by cherry-flavored maraschino liqueur.

1½ ounces gin (I recommend Plymouth)

½ ounce sloe gin (I recommend Plymouth Sloe Gin)

1 teaspoon maraschino liqueur (I recommend Luxardo)

¾ ounce lemon juice

½ ounce berry syrup (page 19)

Crushed ice

Garnish / 2 raspberries and 1 blackberry

Shake both gins, maraschino liqueur, lemon juice, and syrup with cubed ice until chilled.
Strain into a rocks glass filled with crushed ice. To garnish, spear the berries on a pick
and lay it across the rim of the glass.

SYRUPS

When you are preparing a large batch of cocktails for a party, it is often easier to make a syrup with your fruit rather than muddle the fruit into each cocktail. With the Sloe & Low cocktail in this section, for example, a raspberry-blackberry syrup can be made ahead of the party. Unfortunately, herbs don't work the same way. Plants like mint, basil, and shiso lose their luster and brightness of flavor when heated, so as a general rule, I always muddle them into drinks.

Berry Syrup

I love to use berries in cocktails, but they can be a real mess. By making a syrup ahead of time, I can make drinks that capitalize on the flavor without the clean-up. This recipe leaves some room for improvisation. I prefer a mixture of raspberries and blackberries for a rich, tart flavor, but you could also go the route of the purist, using just raspberries or just blackberries. Strawberries and blueberries also work well.

---

1 cup berries of your choosing (for the Sloe & Low on page 17, I use ½ cup blackberries and ½ cup raspberries)

2 cups superfine sugar

1 cup water

In a saucepan, smash the berries into the sugar with a rubber spatula or the back of a spoon, then add water. Heat on low, stirring occasionally, until the sugar is dissolved; this should take no longer than 10 minutes. (Do not let the syrup come to a boil, as you will lose the bright, fresh berry flavor and end up with more of a cooked-berry-pie-tasting syrup.) Take the syrup off the heat and let it sit for 20 minutes. Strain the liquid through a fine-mesh sieve and discard the solids. The syrup will last two weeks in the refrigerator.

MAKES ABOUT 3 CUPS,
enough for about 30 drinks

SANTANA'S SOUR

Hot peppers, like jalapeños and serranos, express their flavors extremely well in the presence of booze. Often too well, for my taste—it can be really difficult to balance such a powerful heat factor in a cocktail. But I love a little spice, so I've worked hard to find the middle ground, and this cocktail is it. Rather than create a syrup, I muddle jalapeño slices to limit the amount of time that the pepper is in contact with the alcohol. By doing this, I can control the spice level and ramp it up for my friends who love an extra-spicy drink. At Clover Club, we often feature a jalapeño-infused tequila, another great way to incorporate peppers into your drinks. You can infuse your own by letting peppers sit in tequila for 8 to 15 minutes, tasting along the way so you can strain out the peppers when you have achieved the spice level you desire.

10 cilantro leaves

4 (1-inch) chunks fresh pineapple

2 wheels (¼-inch) fresh jalapeño, or 3 for a spicier drink

¾ ounce simple syrup

2 ounces blanco tequila (I recommend Don Julio Blanco)

¾ ounce lime juice

Garnish / Pineapple wedge

In the bottom of a shaker, muddle the cilantro, pineapple, and jalapeño with the simple syrup. Add the tequila and lime juice and shake with ice until chilled. Double-strain through a fine-mesh sieve into a double rocks glass filled with ice. To garnish, cut a slit through the bottom of the pineapple wedge and place it on the rim of the glass.

How to Improvise and Make Your Own Cocktails

Once you've made a handful of cocktails from this chapter, I encourage you to start improvising with whatever you've picked up at the market. Try your hand at muddling some vegetables or making syrups with fruit. To help you in your experimenting, I've put together a list of spirits and the fruits and vegetables that they love (not including citrus, which is universally beloved by alcohol).

When creating your bespoke cocktail, keep this golden formula in mind:

2 parts strong (spirit)

¾ parts sour (citrus)

¾ parts sweet (sweetener)

As a rule, this formula will yield a cocktail that is balanced and delicious. Once you have all your ingredients in your shaker, give the combination a taste before you shake it with ice to make sure you're happy with the flavor and balance. And if you plan to top it with sparkling wine or soda water, go heavier on the sugar to account for the dryness of the carbonation.

- **VODKA:** You can't go wrong here. Vodka is polyamorous; it's sort of like the chicken of the cocktail world. It works with pretty much any fruit or vegetable that it meets, so use it to practice with.

- **RUM:** Another spirit with plenty of wiggle room. Berries, passion fruit, guava, mango, coconut, mint, banana, grapes, and pineapple are all good complements.

- **GIN:** Pairs with cucumber, mint, berries, shiso, melon, fennel, apple, kumquat, lemongrass, currants, rosemary, thyme, and sugar snap peas.

- **SHERRY:** Goes well with strawberry, pear, apple, grapes, fig, and apricot.

- **TEQUILA:** A great spirit for more savory ingredients, including tomato, basil, carrot, cilantro, mint, beet, peppers, and celery. Or pair with sweet or tart ingredients such as rhubarb, mango, berries, watermelon, and passion fruit.

- **WHISKEY:** Goes well with mint, berries, peach, cherry, apricot, plum, fig, and apple.

Blush Baby

As anyone who's ever been to a beach resort can tell you, rum and fruit are a natural pair. The caramel-like sugars in Flor de Caña and Appleton Estate rums offer amazing depth when combined with the berry fruit.

1 blackberry

1 raspberry

¾ ounce demerara syrup (page 23)

1¼ ounces white rum (I recommend Flor de Caña Extra Dry 4 Year)

½ ounce Jamaican rum (I recommend Appleton Estate V/X)

½ ounce lemon juice

2 ounces dry or sparkling rosé wine

Crushed ice

Garnish / 1 blackberry and 1 raspberry

In the bottom of a shaker, muddle the berries in the syrup. Add the rums and lemon juice and shake with cubed ice until chilled. Double-strain through a fine-mesh sieve into a wine goblet filled with crushed ice. Top with the rosé. Spear the berries on a pick and lay it across the rim of the glass to garnish.

Demerara Syrup

Demerara sugar is a large-grained sugar with origins in
Guyana. It's not as refined as granulated sugar and has a natural
caramel-like flavor. I like to use demerara in cocktails with
brown spirits. Note that this syrup has a ratio of 2:1 sugar to
water and will be sweeter than a basic 1:1 simple syrup.

1 cup demerara sugar

½ cup water

In a saucepan over medium heat,
combine the sugar and water. Cook,
stirring, until the sugar dissolves,
taking care not to let the mixture
boil. Remove from heat, let cool,
and transfer the syrup to a container
with a lid and refrigerate it. The
syrup will last one month in the
refrigerator.

MAKES ABOUT 1 CUP,
enough for about 10 drinks

2

Fourth of July

It has become something of a tradition for me to spend the Fourth of July with booze writer and historian David Wondrich. Dave is the world's foremost expert on the history of the American cocktail, and he advised me on the opening of Clover Club. When I was thinking about opening the bar in Brooklyn, Dave, a lifelong Brooklynite, convinced me that Smith Street would be the best location. I took his advice and found a space in Carroll Gardens. Later, he admitted that his motives had been somewhat selfish—he wanted a cocktail bar that he could walk to!—but Smith Street ended up being the perfect place for our pre-Prohibition-style bar.

Dave throws a massive barbecue in his backyard each year, and it has grown into an annual gathering of New York's cocktail industry—a day when we can get away from our bars and enjoy sunshine, sausage, and one of Dave's famous punches. Dave's friends include writers, chefs, recipe testers, bar owners, and mixologists— it's a lively crowd that makes for a great party. When things are in full swing, Dave leads us all in a reading of the Declaration of Independence. Copies are dispersed and each guest recites a line or two, which is quite a challenge when you've consumed several glasses of punch!

When I can't make it to Dave's, I use the holiday as an excuse to get patriotic with my cocktailing by focusing on classically American spirits like rye or applejack. In addition, I always keep refreshing ingredients like soda water and citrus on hand to fight the inevitable heat of a New York summer.

In this chapter I've included several large-format punches as well as a primer on batching. The recipes were created with summer in mind, but the techniques are worth bookmarking for all seasons and will save you lots of time when hosting larger groups.

SPREAD EAGLE PUNCH

MAKES 18 SERVINGS

This recipe comes directly from David Wondrich's Fourth of July bash. He wrote the book on punch—and I mean that literally; his book, *Punch,* gives an in-depth history of this style of drink—so there is always at least one bowl of the stuff on hand.

Peels of 12 lemons

1 cup turbinado sugar

12 cups water, divided

1½ (750-ml) bottles rye whiskey (Dave recommends Rittenhouse)

1½ (750-ml) bottles blended Scotch (Dave recommends Black Grouse)

Large ice block (see headnote on page 27)

Garnish / Lemon wheels (from 8 lemons) and nutmeg

Place the lemon peels in a large bowl. Add the sugar to the lemon peels and muddle until the sugar looks slightly moistened. Cover and let sit for an hour.

Bring 1 cup of the water to a boil. Pour the boiling water over the lemon peel mixture and stir until sugar has dissolved. Add the whiskeys and the remaining 11 cups water and chill. To serve, transfer the punch to a punch bowl. Right before serving, fish out the lemon peels with a slotted spoon and add the large ice block. Garnish by placing the lemon wheels in the punch and grating nutmeg over the surface.

 **PRO TIP** | *You will want to make your lemon peels as long as possible so they are easier to remove when the time comes.*

BOATHOUSE PUNCH

MAKES 20 SERVINGS

At the bar, we have giant ice molds to make the ice cubes that keep this punch cold, but when I do it at home, a Tupperware container works just as well. Fill a 1-quart to 2-quart container with hot water (which freezes into clearer ice) and stick it in the freezer twenty-four hours before the party. Then add the giant cube to your punch bowl right before the guests arrive; it keeps everything cold and looks beautiful.

Peels of 4 lemons

½ cup superfine sugar

1 (1-liter) bottle gin (I recommend Bombay Dry or Bombay Sapphire)

1 (750-ml) bottle Aperol

12 ounces St. Germain elderflower liqueur

12 ounces lemon juice

12 ounces orange juice

12 ounces grapefruit juice

Large ice block

1 (750-ml) bottle sparkling rosé wine

Garnish / Lemon wheels (from 2 lemons)

Place the lemon peels in a bowl with the sugar (save the lemons for juicing). Muddle the peels until the sugar looks slightly moistened, then let sit covered for at least 1 hour, or overnight.

In a large punch bowl, combine the gin, Aperol, St. Germain, and juices. Add the lemon peel mixture and let sit for 15 minutes. Remove the peels. Right before serving, add the ice block and rosé. Garnish the punch bowl with the lemon wheels.

Dilution and Chilling

Ice is an essential ingredient in any cocktail; we use it to dilute and also to chill. By shaking or stirring a cocktail with ice, we introduce 1 to 1½ ounces of water into the cocktail (about 25 percent of the total volume). The change in dilution and temperature brings out the subtleties of the spirit and helps to meld the flavors together.

For the best results, you should start with spirits at room temperature. Some people keep vodka and gin in the freezer, but I don't recommend it: You won't get the proper level of dilution when you add ice to your cocktail. Juices and wine-based aperitifs, however, should be stored in the refrigerator to preserve them.

When stirring a cocktail, be sure to fill your mixing glass all the way with ice. The bar spoon should go to the bottom of the glass so that you do not agitate the drink. A stirred cocktail should be silky, smooth, and free of air bubbles. You will know your cocktail is ready when the corners of your ice cubes have a rounded look and the glass is frosted. This will take approximately 20 to 25 seconds.

When shaking a cocktail, you will want to feel a frost on the outside of the mixing tin, which should develop after approximately 15 seconds of vigorous shaking.

When I make cocktails with crushed ice at home, I use a Lewis bag. These canvas bags have been around a long time, and unlike mechanical ice crushers, they don't break! Simply place your ice cubes into the bag and hit them with a muddler or mallet. There are quite a few on the market, but I recommend the TAG Bar Lewis bag.

Jersey Julep

Juleps, tiny mountains of crushed ice with flags of refreshing mint leaves, are made for the height of summer. And the ice might be the most important ingredient of all; without it, the drink won't have the right water content and will be unbalanced. Adding the ice in three parts ensures that the cocktail will be just diluted enough.

8 to 10 mint leaves

½ ounce grade B maple syrup

2 ounces bonded apple brandy (I recommend Laird's)

Crushed ice

Garnish / 2 to 3 mint sprigs

In the bottom of a julep cup, gently muddle the mint in the maple syrup, just enough to release the oils in the mint leaves. Add the brandy and fill the cup halfway with crushed ice. Stir until chilled (the cup should become frosty), then add more ice, stir again, and then pack the top with a cone of ice. Garnish with the mint sprigs placed next to the straw for maximum aromatic appeal.

KEEPING DRINKS COOL

If you're hosting an outdoor party in the warmer months, consider serving your punch from a cooler (like an Igloo with a spigot at the bottom) or an ice chest. It will keep the punch cool without diluting it too much.

SOUTHLAND SIPPER

This cocktail falls into a category I like to call porch drinks (or stoop drinks, for those of us who live in Brooklyn). On a humid summer day on the East Coast, I am looking for a long drink that is really going to quench my thirst. This one does the trick.

1 strawberry, hulled

¾ ounce simple syrup

1½ ounces rye whiskey (I recommend Wild Turkey 101)

¼ ounce Bénédictine

¾ ounce lemon juice

2 dashes Angostura bitters

2 ounces club soda

Garnish / I strawberry, halved, and a spiral lemon twist

In the bottom of a shaker, muddle the strawberry in the simple syrup. Add the rye, Bénédictine, lemon juice, and bitters and shake with ice. Double-strain through a fine-mesh sieve into a Collins glass over fresh ice and top with the club soda. Garnish with the strawberry and spiral lemon twist.

OLEO SACCHA-WHAT?

The very simple technique of muddling citrus peels and sugar together and letting it sit for a while (as seen in the earlier punch recipes) results in a product with a very fancy, Harry Potter–sounding name: *oleo saccharum.* It's Latin for "sugared oil," which is exactly what you're making: The essential oils in the peels of the citrus dissolve the sugar into a flavor-packed slurry that will upgrade any punch. The effect is the punch equivalent of expressing the oils of a twist over a drink.

Ginger-Mint Lemonade

The ginger syrup in this drink is the real star. It's so good, in fact, that you could leave the booze out entirely for an undeniably delicious mocktail.

8 mint leaves

¾ ounce ginger syrup (page 33)

2 ounces citrus vodka or gin (I recommend Ketel One Citroen or Tanqueray No. Ten)

¾ ounce lemon juice

1½ ounces water

Garnish / Mint sprig

In the bottom of a shaker, muddle the mint leaves with the ginger syrup. Add the vodka or gin, lemon juice, and water and shake with ice until chilled. Strain into a Collins glass filled with ice and garnish with the mint sprig.

Ginger Syrup

Ginger is a very versatile cocktail ingredient. It works with any spirit category and adds spice to your beverage without adding heat. It's essential to categories of drinks called "mules" and "bucks," most frequently encountered in the form of the Moscow Mule. The best way to make it is with a juice extractor (used to juice vegetables and noncitrus fruits). If you don't have one, you can still make ginger juice with a bit of elbow grease: Just grate fresh peeled ginger root with a microplane zester and then squeeze it through a piece of cheesecloth. However, when you're entertaining or making lots of drinks, it's perfectly acceptable to buy a bottled ginger juice or syrup. There are quite a few good ones on the market today. I recommend ginger juice from the Ginger People and Hawaiian ginger syrup from Pacifikool, both of which can be found online.

½ cup ginger juice

I cup superfine sugar

Heat the juice in a saucepan over low heat until warm but not boiling. Add the sugar and blend with an immersion blender or whisk. Let cool, then transfer to a nonreactive metal or glass container with a lid and store in the refrigerator for up to three weeks.

MAKES ABOUT I CUP,
enough for about 13 drinks

Moscow Mule

Though this drink is traditionally made with vodka, the beauty of the mule is that the formula works with any spirit. Substitute dark rum, tequila, or gin for the vodka for a delicious variation on the classic. Or try it with whiskey or Scotch, swapping out the lime juice for lemon juice.

2 ounces vodka (I recommend Stoli)

¾ ounce ginger syrup (page 33)

¾ ounce lime juice

Club soda

Garnish / Candied ginger and lime wheel

Shake the vodka, ginger syrup, and lime juice with ice until chilled. Strain into a rocks glass filled with ice and fill to the top with club soda. To make the garnish, spear the candied ginger and the lime wheel with a toothpick and perch on the rim of the glass.

BATCHING

"Batching" is industry-speak for preparing cocktails in larger yields, and it's common practice when making drinks for big groups. Trust me, you don't want to stand around mixing one drink at a time when you're entertaining more than ten guests. You've probably already come into contact with a batched drink: Punches are the most popular example. In fact, many of the drinks in this book are easily batched. Here, I've outlined the basics of batching, including calculating ingredient amounts, diluting, and batching no-no's. Stick to these guidelines and you'll be a batching wizard.

UNDERSTAND YOUR PROPORTIONS

There are a number of ways to batch drinks.

- Get out the calculator and multiply the ounces listed in the recipe by the number of drinks you wish to make. This is the most precise way of batching at home, in my opinion.

- Wherever you see "ounces" in a recipe, change it to "cups." This increases your yield from one serving to eight servings.

- Figure out the ratio. For example, if you are batching a drink composed of 1½ ounces gin, ¾ ounce Campari, and ¾ ounce vermouth, you have proportions of 2:1:1. You can then batch by any volume you wish, as long as that ratio between gin, Campari, and vermouth remains the same.

SHAKEN VERSUS STIRRED

There isn't a great batching workaround for cocktails that call for being shaken. You can mix the ingredients ahead of time, but you will still need to shake the batched mixture one cocktail at a time. Still, having your ingredients premixed in a large volume does save you the time of measuring things out over and over again.

The easiest recipes to batch are stirred cocktails. Instead of stirring, simply add 25 percent of the batch's total volume in water and chill in the refrigerator before serving. The water will dilute the drink approximately as much as stirring it with ice would. Some cocktail purists believe this method does not get the drink cold enough, and if your refrigerator isn't at the right temperature, they could be right. Be sure to chill the vessel that you are serving the drink in to avoid a warm cocktail.

INGREDIENTS WE NEVER BATCH

Always add these ingredients at the last minute, right before serving the cocktail:

- BITTERS: Bitters tend to intensify when added to a batch of cocktails, making them overly bitter.

- BUBBLES: Soda water, tonic, and sparkling wine are best saved until the final moment; if you add them early, they will go flat.

- EGGS: If you're batching fizzes or flips (both shaken drinks), add the egg or egg white as you're shaking the drink. For example, if you were batching a Clover Club cocktail (page 128), you would batch your gin, dry vermouth, raspberry syrup, and lemon juice. When you were ready to shake up the drink, you would add 3 ounces of your batch to your mixing glass and add ½ ounce of egg white.

WHEN YOU'RE READY TO SERVE

The biggest advantage of batching is that you can do it ahead of your event, creating a major time save while you're entertaining.

If you've premixed your batch and let it sit for more than thirty minutes, make sure to give it a good stir before you serve it or add individual portions to your shaker; sugar is heavier than citrus juice and booze and will sink to the bottom of the mixture, making your last few cocktails overly sweet.

A final note about batching in advance: Some ingredients, especially liqueurs and bitter spirits, will expand and intensify in flavor when left to sit in a batch. If a recipe calls for maraschino liqueur, Campari, absinthe, or Chartreuse, for example, add less than the recipe calls for at the time of preparation. When you're ready to serve, you can adjust and add more if you'd like.

Here are a handful of drinks that I frequently batch:

NEGRONI

Makes 10 drinks

15 ounces gin (I recommend Tanqueray)
10 ounces Campari
10 ounces sweet vermouth (I recommend Martini)
8³⁄₄ ounces cold water

Garnish / ORANGE PEELS (FROM 1 ORANGE)

In a large container, combine the gin, Campari, sweet vermouth, and water, and stir well. Chill in the refrigerator until very cold, at least 2 hours. To make one serving, pour about 4 ounces of the batch into a Martini glass and add an orange peel to garnish. (If you want to serve this as a pitcher drink, simply combine the ingredients in a pitcher with some ice and leave it out next to some glasses for guests to help themselves.)

HEMINGWAY DAIQUIRI

Makes 10 drinks

20 ounces rum (white rum is the standard and I recommend Bacardi Heritage; but it's also delicious with Santa Teresa 1796, an aged rum)
5 ounces maraschino liqueur (I recommend Luxardo)
7¹⁄₂ ounces lime juice
7¹⁄₂ ounces grapefruit juice
5 ounces simple syrup

 *Garnish* / LIME WHEELS (FROM ABOUT 2 LIMES)

In a large container, combine the rum, maraschino liqueur, lime juice, grapefruit juice, and simple syrup (this can be prepared up to 12 hours ahead of time and stored in the refrigerator). To make one serving, place 4½ ounces of the batch in a cocktail shaker and shake with ice until chilled. Strain into a cocktail glass and garnish with a lime wheel placed on top of the drink.

MARGARITA

Makes 10 drinks

20 ounces blanco tequila (I recommend El Tesoro)
7¹⁄₂ ounces Cointreau
7¹⁄₂ ounces lime juice
2¹⁄₂ ounces simple syrup

Garnish / LIME WHEELS (FROM 2 LIMES)

In a large container, combine the tequila, Cointreau, lime juice, and simple syrup (this can be prepared up to 12 hours ahead of time and stored in the refrigerator). To make one serving, place 3¾ ounces of the batch in a cocktail shaker and shake with ice until chilled. Strain into a rocks glass filled with ice and garnish with a lime wheel placed on top of the drink.

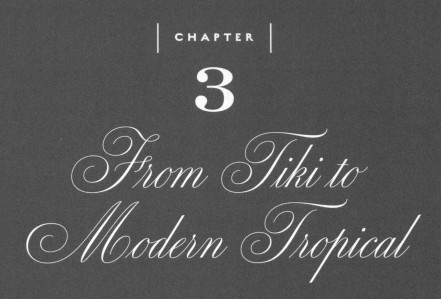

3

From Tiki to Modern Tropical

Being from Hawaii, I am constantly asked about tiki drinks. Many people are under the impression that this style of drink came out of the island culture in Hawaii, when in fact it was the invention of a few California boys. The faux-tropical craze originated in the 1930s at Don the Beachcomber, a bar and restaurant in Hollywood, California. But it really took off about a decade later with "Trader Vic" Bergeron and many others who loved the exotic drinks and Polynesian décor. They are served in elaborate vessels and adorned with over-the-top garnishes.

In 2010, I opened a modern tropical cocktail lounge called Lani Kai in New York City that embraced the brilliance of these classic tiki drinks within a more modern expression. Most tiki cocktails feature a blend of rums. At Lani Kai we paired tropical ingredients with a wider spread of spirits, including gin, bourbon, tequila, and pisco, and served them in modern glassware.

On Monday nights at Lani Kai, we brought in Brian Miller, a bartender and tiki aficionado who cut his teeth at Pegu Club and Death & Co. (both hugely popular cocktail bars in New York), to do a raucous event called Tiki Monday. Brian and his pirate crew took over the basement bar of Lani Kai for an evening of Scorpion Bowls, Zombies, and other interpretations of the tiki classics. The night became an industry favorite with a revolving cast of celebrity bartenders, including King Cocktail himself, Dale DeGroff.

Whether modern or classic, tropical drinks just make you feel good. They are liquid vacations, the next best thing to a plane ticket, and a great theme around which to gather a few friends.

TIKI PARTY TIPS

The drinks in this chapter are excellent for entertaining because they are colorful, festive, and thoroughly delicious. Use them as the centerpiece of a tiki- or Hawaiian-themed party on a hot summer day. Here are a few tips for setting the mood.

- **MUSIC:** There are plenty of compilations out there. Look for the *Hawaii Five-0* theme, "Tiny Bubbles," or "(Put the Lime in the) Coconut" for a fun kitsch feel, or Martin Denny's "Hypnotique" and "Swamp Fire" for a more ultra-lounge feel. For classic Hawaiiana, look for songs like "Waikiki," "Sweet Leilani," "Honolulu City Lights," or anything by the artist Israel "Iz" Kamakawiwo'ole.

- **WARDROBE:** Aloha shirts, muumuus, vintage tiki dresses, and flower leis.

- **PROPS:** Grass skirts, ti or banana leaves, blow-up palm trees, bowls of tropical fruit, tiki torches. You can find great table decorations, such as lei garlands, tabletop torches, and more at orientaltrading.com. For classic Hawaiiana go with real flower leis; they're pricey but worth it. Try www .hawaiianleicompany.com.

- **BARWARE:** Ceramic tiki mugs, scorpion bowls, colorful straws, miniature umbrellas, back scratchers, hollowed-out pineapples and coconuts. Peruse the large selection of tiki mugs and scorpion bowls at retroplanet.com, and check out orientaltrading.com for the straws and umbrellas.

If you're making cocktails for a group of four to eight, consider these cocktails:

- Pacific Swizzle (page 48)
- Pele's Wrath (page 64)

If you're making cocktails for a group of eight to twelve, consider these cocktails:

- Sugarhill Gang (page 54)
- Summer Negroni (page 41)

If you're making cocktails for a group larger than twelve, consider these cocktails:

- Hanalei Sun (page 45)
- Hawaiian Iced Tea (page 51)

INFUSIONS

If you've never tried to make an infusion at home, you're missing out. The technique of soaking different ingredients in spirits and then straining them out might seem like a lot of effort for a cocktail, but really it just takes a bit of patience. The rewards will last you several rounds.

Spirits can be infused with fruit, herbs, spices, vegetables, and teas. As a general rule, fruit will need the most time to infuse, between four and seven days. Herbs, spices, and teas will take the least time to infuse, generally between fifteen and forty-five minutes. When using ingredients with very strong flavors, such as hot peppers, spices, and teas, make sure to taste the infusion every five minutes so that you can strain it when you have achieved the flavor you want.

For first-time infusions, I'd start with vodka, which picks up flavors fast (why do you think there are so many flavored vodkas out there?), and the fruit of your choice.

Once you get comfortable with that, the sky is the limit: You can infuse fruit into gin or coffee into Campari. You can even infuse bacon fat into bourbon in a technique called fat-washing. A word to the wise: Don't be tempted to snack on the fruit you've used in an infusion. The booze leaches all of the fruit's flavor, leaving only the sharp bite of alcohol in its wake.

A note about preparing and storing infusions: You'll need a large container to hold your infusion ingredients while they do their magic. Stick to metal or glass, which are nonreactive and won't pick up any of the flavors (unlike plastic).

Hanalei Sun, Apple-Infused Vodka, and Strawberry-Infused Aperol

SUMMER NEGRONI

The classic Negroni (page 37) is one of my favorite cocktails, but it can be a bit heavy for a warm summer afternoon. This version is light and bright and well-suited to a picnic blanket.

1 ounce gin (I recommend Bombay Dry)

1 ounce strawberry-infused Aperol (page 43)

1 ounce bianco vermouth
(I recommend Martini; you can use sweet vermouth if you don't have bianco)

Garnish / Orange slice

In a mixing glass, combine the gin, infused Aperol, and vermouth. Add ice and stir until chilled. Strain into a chilled rocks glass filled with ice. Garnish with the orange slice in the glass.

BLONDE REDHEAD

A couple years ago, I had made an Aperol infusion for a farmers'
market charity event and had some left over. When I came back to the bar
after working the event, exhausted and thirsty, one of my bartenders and
I took the leftover infusion and started making a "kitchen sink" cocktail—
adding whatever was handy. The result was shockingly delicious—so much
so that we added it to the bar menu.

3 ounces strawberry-infused Aperol (page 43)

1 ounce grapefruit juice

¼ ounce lemon juice

1 to 3 ounces soda water

Garnish / Orange twist or strawberry

In a Collins glass filled with ice, combine the
infused Aperol, grapefruit juice, and lemon juice.
Fill to the rim with soda water and stir once or
twice to combine. Garnish with the orange twist or
strawberry (or both).

Strawberry-Infused Aperol

Aperol, the low-alcohol cousin of Campari, is an Italian aperitif with a slightly bittersweet orange flavor. As soon as strawberries come into season, I make this infusion, which gives the Aperol a tart brightness. When I've gone to the trouble of making strawberry-infused Aperol, I end up using it in pretty much everything (it's that delicious). Two cocktails here, the Blonde Redhead (page 42) and the Summer Negroni (page 41), are my favorite ways to put it to use. And for a simple brunch drink, you can mix a few ounces with sparkling wine or soda water and serve over ice.

1 pint strawberries, hulled and cut into quarters

1 (750-ml) bottle Aperol

In a large nonreactive metal or glass container with a lid, combine the strawberries and Aperol. Cover and let sit in the refrigerator for 4 days, stirring it once a day, then strain through a fine-mesh sieve set over a bowl, discarding the fruit. Funnel the infusion back into the original bottle and label. The Aperol infusion will keep for two weeks in the refrigerator.

MAKES ABOUT 3 CUPS,
enough for 8 to 24 drinks

HANALEI SUN

MAKES ABOUT 3 CUPS, ENOUGH FOR 7 DRINKS

This is one of the simplest recipes in the book and one of the first drinks people gravitate toward when I put it out at a party. Named for Hanalei (pronounced *hawn-ah-lay*) Bay on the north shore of Kauai, it's a great first-time infusion experiment. It does require a bit of lead time, however: The mixture must sit for at least one week for maximum flavor, so plan accordingly.

I pineapple, peeled, cored, and cut into 1-inch pieces

I (750-ml) bottle vodka or white rum

Garnish / Pineapple wedges, I per serving

Place the pineapple pieces and the vodka or rum in a large nonreactive metal or glass container with a lid. Cover and let sit for one week in the refrigerator, stirring it once a day. Strain the liquid through a fine-mesh sieve set over a bowl, allowing the fruit to sit in the strainer for 30 minutes so as to get all the liquid. Discard the fruit and funnel the infusion back into the original bottle and label. The infusion will keep for two weeks in the refrigerator.

To serve, pour 3½ ounces of the pineapple infusion into a shaker and shake with ice until chilled. Strain into a chilled coupe glass and garnish with a pineapple wedge.

PRO TIP

Oftentimes infused spirits go down super easily. But be careful: This drink is just as strong as a Martini, despite its light and bright flavor. Drink responsibly.

Tea in Cocktails

I love using tea in cocktails. The tannins offer depth and controlled bitterness and pair with fruit beautifully. Tea is also great for infusions: Just steep a few tea bags in a bottle of vodka or rum, and you have an entirely different ingredient to work with. But take care not to oversteep or your drink will be too bitter.

Passion Fruit Tea-Infused Rum

Makes about 4 cups, enough for about 16 drinks

The tropical notes in passion fruit tea marry beautifully with the buttery caramel notes of rum. This infusion is a great way to add bright, beachy flavors to a cocktail without loading it down with sugar.

1 (1-liter) bottle white rum (I recommend Bacardi Heritage)
4 bags passion fruit tea (I like Tazo brand)

In a large nonreactive metal or glass container, combine the tea bags and the rum. Let steep for 40 minutes at room temperature, then remove the tea bags, funnel the liquid back into the original bottle, and label. The infusion will keep for two weeks in the refrigerator.

Once you've made the passion fruit tea infusion, there are a number of ways to use it. It's brilliant when mixed with lemonade (like a boozy Arnold Palmer), or in a slightly more involved drink such as the Summer Daze (page 47) or the Pacific Swizzle (page 48).

SUMMER DAZE

The next time you cut up a pineapple (whether for snacking or for juicing),
hold on to the top. Those leaves make lovely garnishes.

1½ ounces passion fruit tea–infused rum (page 46)

½ ounce Campari

½ ounce lime juice

¾ ounce pineapple juice

¾ ounce simple syrup

2 ounces club soda

Garnish / Pineapple leaf

Shake the tea-infused rum, Campari, lime juice, pineapple juice, and simple syrup with
ice until chilled. Strain into a Collins glass filled with ice and top with club soda. To
garnish, place the pineapple leaf in the glass.

Pacific Swizzle

The swizzle is a celebration of ice. This style of drink originated in the Caribbean, shortly after ice production had made its way to the islands. By blending crushed ice, alcohol, and sugar in a glass with a swizzle stick (traditionally a forked stick made from a root), you create a delightful, refreshing grown-up slushy.

2 ounces passion fruit tea-infused rum (page 46)

¾ ounce simple syrup

½ ounce lime juice

¼ ounce passion fruit puree (available in specialty stores or online at gourmetfoodstore.com)

Crushed ice

Garnish / Orchid and orange half wheel

Combine the rum, simple syrup, lime juice, and puree in a Collins glass; fill the glass a third full with crushed ice and swizzle (see "Swizzling" sidebar below) using a swizzle stick or bar spoon. Add more crushed ice to about one inch below the lip of the glass; swizzle again in the top half of the glass. Pack with additional crushed ice and garnish with the orchid and the orange half wheel.

Swizzling

To properly swizzle a cocktail, fill a glass one third full with crushed ice. Insert a swizzle stick or bar spoon all the way to the bottom of the glass. Hold the top of the stick or spoon between the palms of your hands and roll it back and forth quickly (like trying to start a campfire). Simultaneously, move the stick vertically up to the surface of the ice and back down to the bottom of the glass. Slowly add crushed ice and repeat the process until the outside of the glass is frosty and the glass is filled. Remove the swizzle stick and cap the drink off with a cone of ice.

Hawaiian Iced Tea

This cocktail is more complicated than most in this book, but I think it's worth the extra effort. And it makes a wonderful party pitcher drink. Once you prepare the infusion and the syrup, it comes together in a flash.

2 ounces tea-infused orange vodka (page 52)

½ ounce lemon juice

¾ ounce mint tea simple syrup (page 53)

2 ounces water

Garnish / Lemon wheel and mint sprig

In a Collins glass filled with ice, combine the infused vodka, lemon juice, simple syrup, and water. Roll the drink to mix, then place the lemon wheel on the surface of the drink and add the mint sprig to garnish.

Tea-Infused Orange Vodka

This recipe is based on the very first tea infusion I ever attempted. I had fallen in love with the Lili'uokalani tea and was experimenting with different ways to incorporate it into a cocktail. At first, I was brewing iced tea and adding it to the vodka separately, but the process didn't deliver the concentrated tea flavor I was after. By steeping the tea directly in the vodka, the bright floral notes of the tea really come through.

---

1 (1-liter) bottle orange vodka (I recommend Stoli Ohranj)

5 tablespoons loose black tea (I recommend SerendipiTea's Lili'uokalani, a tropical black tea with mango and guava notes)

In a nonreactive metal or glass container, combine the vodka and the tea and let steep at room temperature for 30 to 40 minutes, until the mixture takes on a dark brown color. Strain the liquid through a fine-mesh sieve set over a bowl, discarding the tea. Funnel the infusion back into the original bottle and label. The infusion will keep for three weeks in the refrigerator.

MAKES ABOUT 4 CUPS,
enough for about 16 drinks

Mint Tea Simple Syrup

Remember how I said that delicate herbs don't make for great syrups? Herbal teas provide a great workaround. I keep this syrup around as my standard sweetener for iced tea; it's also delicious in iced lemonade.

1½ cups boiling water

1½ tablespoons loose mint tea

1½ cups granulated sugar

In a nonreactive metal or glass container, pour the boiling water over the mint tea and let steep for 10 minutes. Strain the liquid through a fine-mesh sieve set over a bowl, then add the sugar to the liquid and stir until dissolved. Store in a nonreactive metal or glass container with a lid in the refrigerator for up to one week.

MAKES 2¼ CUPS,
enough for about 24 drinks

SUGARHILL GANG

My favorite tiki pirate, Brian Miller, is behind this whimsical drink. Orgeat is an almond syrup that appears in many tiki recipes, most famously the Mai Tai. It's sort of a pain to make from scratch, so I recommend buying a high-quality prepared version, like the one from Orgeat Works, which is available at orgeatworks.com.

1½ ounces aged rum (Brian recommends Appleton Estate Reserve)

½ ounce Calvados (Brian recommends Busnel VSOP)

½ ounce lemon juice

½ ounce orange juice

½ ounce orgeat (I recommend T'Orgeat from Orgeat Works)

1 teaspoon cinnamon syrup (page 55)

Garnish / Lemon wheel

Shake the rum, Calvados, lemon juice, orange juice, orgeat, and cinnamon syrup with ice until chilled. Strain into a cocktail glass and garnish with the lemon wheel.

SYRUPS FROM SPICES

Syrups go way beyond fruit. In tiki culture, syrups are a common conveyance for adding the flavor of certain spices to drinks. Spices, after all, share an origin with many of the tropical fruits that star in tiki recipes.

I keep an array of infused syrups in my refrigerator, as part of my "entertaining life raft." If surprise guests drop in and I don't have time to prepare anything super complicated, I fall back on these syrups to make a dead-easy cocktail that smacks of sophistication. They are also great for mocktails and make excellent upgrades to iced tea or sparkling water.

Cinnamon Syrup

Baking spices played a big role in early tiki drinks. Donn Beach of Don the Beachcomber used cinnamon, vanilla, and allspice in his secret spice blends, simply labeled Don's Spices #2 and #4 to protect the formulas. Many modern tropical libations take their inspiration from those early spiced syrups.

If you want to geek out about syrups like I do, I recommend using cassia cinnamon bark (available at zamourispices.com) as it has a higher oil content than regular cinnamon, making for a more intense flavor. But regular cinnamon sticks will still make a delicious syrup.

½ ounce cassia cinnamon bark or 5 cinnamon sticks

1 cup superfine sugar

1 cup water

In a saucepan, muddle the cinnamon bark into tiny pieces. Add the sugar and water and heat over medium heat, stirring periodically so the sugar doesn't burn and stick to the pan. Bring to a boil, then cover, reduce heat, and simmer for about 5 minutes. Remove from heat, keep covered, and let sit overnight in the refrigerator. Strain the syrup through a fine-mesh sieve into a nonreactive metal or glass container with a lid. The syrup will keep for about one month in the refrigerator.

MAKES 1½ CUPS,
enough for about 20 drinks

MAI TAI

The Mai Tai is by far the most iconic drink to come out of the tiki craze. This 1944 version was created by Trader Vic at his flagship bar in Oakland, California. Recipes were kept under wraps at most tiki dens, causing bartenders elsewhere to make up their own versions upon the request of a patron. I have been served many a tropical drink under the moniker Mai Tai, and while they are usually delicious, they are usually *not* Mai Tais! Vic's recipe is boozy, citrusy, and strong…and not red or blue!

1 ounce Martinique rum (I recommend Clément VSOP)

1 ounce Jamaican rum (I recommend Appleton Estate Reserve)

½ ounce orange curaçao (I recommend Pierre Ferrand Dry)

¾ ounce lime juice

¼ ounce orgeat (I recommend T'Orgeat from Orgeat Works)

¼ ounce simple syrup

Crushed ice

Garnish / Traditionally, just a mint sprig, but I serve mine with a lime wheel and an orchid as well.

Shake the rums, orange curaçao, lime juice, orgeat, and simple syrup with cubed ice until chilled. Strain into a rocks glass filled with crushed ice. Garnish with the mint sprig and add the lime wheel and orchid, if using.

GOLD COAST

Allspice is another flavor frequently encountered in the world of tropical drinks. Here, instead of going through the trouble of making an allspice syrup, I use Dale DeGroff's aromatic allspice bitters.

2 ounces aged rum (I recommend Bacardi 8)

¾ ounce pineapple juice

¾ ounce lime juice

1 ounce simple syrup

2 dashes Dale DeGroff's Pimento bitters (available at cocktailkingdom.com)

2 ounces sparkling wine (I recommend Moët & Chandon Impérial or Gruet Brut)

Garnish / Lime wheel and pineapple leaf

Shake the rum, pineapple juice, lime juice, simple syrup, and bitters with ice until chilled. Strain into a wineglass filled with ice. Top with the sparkling wine and garnish with the lime wheel and pineapple leaf in the glass.

BLUE HAWAII

A tiki party wouldn't be complete without a blue drink, and the Blue Hawaii (also known as the Blue Hawaiian, depending on whom you ask) is one of my favorites. It was created in 1957 by Harry Yee, legendary head bartender at the Hilton Hawaiian Village in Waikiki, when a sales representative of Dutch distiller Bols asked him to design a drink that featured their blue curaçao liqueur. This is my version of his classic.

1½ ounces white rum (I recommend El Dorado 3 Year)

½ ounce blue curaçao

1 ounce pineapple juice

½ ounce lemon juice

¼ ounce simple syrup

1 teaspoon cream of coconut (I recommend Calahua or Coco Lopez)

Crushed ice

Garnish / Orange slice and orchid

Shake the rum, curaçao, pineapple juice, lemon juice, simple syrup, and cream of coconut with 3 ice cubes until chilled. Strain into a hurricane glass filled with crushed ice. To garnish, place the orange slice on the rim of the glass and tuck the orchid into the ice at the top of the glass.

Thai Daiquiri

There are few things as perfect as a Daiquiri. The three-ingredient cocktail is an exercise in simplicity. But when I have some lemongrass syrup on hand, I like to swap it in for regular simple syrup; the change is subtle but beguiling, and great for a summer evening. Take it a step farther by muddling three or four leaves of Thai basil in the shaker before adding the other ingredients.

2 ounces white rum (I recommend Banks 5 Island)

¾ ounce lime juice

¾ ounce lemongrass syrup (page 62)

Garnish / 1 (3-inch) piece lemongrass stalk and 1 lime wheel

Shake the rum, lime juice, and lemongrass syrup with ice until chilled. Strain into a Martini glass. To garnish, spear the lime wheel with the lemongrass stalk and rest inside the glass.

Lemongrass Syrup

Tropical, fragrant, and subtle, lemongrass is one of my favorite ingredients. This syrup is much more "modern tropical" than tiki, and it goes way beyond cocktails. Try drizzling it over fruit or letting it soak into coconut cake.

10 stalks lemongrass, ends trimmed and brittle outer layers removed (available at Whole Foods or other specialty markets)

2 cups water

Granulated sugar

Puree the lemongrass in a food processor and transfer to a saucepan. Add the water and simmer over medium heat until the mixture is reduced by half. Remove from heat and let cool. Transfer to the refrigerator and let sit overnight.

Strain the lemongrass water through a fine-mesh sieve into a bowl, discarding the lemongrass pulp. Measure the infused water and place in a saucepan. Add an equal amount of granulated sugar (it should be about 1 cup) and cook over medium heat, stirring until the sugar dissolves. Let cool completely and transfer to a nonreactive metal or glass container with a lid. The syrup will keep for up to two weeks in the refrigerator.

MAKES 1½ CUPS,
enough for about 17 drinks

Leilani's Fizz

Lychees don't have much of a following here in the States, but I grew up eating them like candy and absolutely love the way they taste in cocktails. If you can't find fresh lychee nuts, increase the amount of lychee juice to 1½ ounces.

---

2 fresh or canned lychee nuts

2 ounces gin (I recommend Tanqueray)

1 ounce lychee juice

½ ounce lime juice

¾ ounce lemongrass syrup (page 62)

1½ ounces soda water

Garnish / 1 (3-inch) piece lemongrass stalk and 1 lime wheel

In the bottom of a shaker, muddle the lychee nuts. Add the gin, lychee juice, lime juice, and lemongrass syrup and shake with ice until chilled. Strain into a Collins glass filled with ice and top with the soda water. To garnish, spear the lime wheel with the lemongrass stalk and rest inside the glass.

PELE'S WRATH

In Hawaii, Pele is the goddess of fire; she's the one who causes volcanoes to erupt. When I was creating a cocktail menu for the Andaz Wailea in Maui, I wanted to include this drink, but the cultural advisor, Kainoa, insisted that we change the name so as not to anger Pele.

2 ounces blanco tequila (I recommend Don Julio)

½ ounce Aperol

1 ounce pineapple juice

¾ ounce lime juice

½ ounce grenadine (page 66)

Crushed ice

Garnish / Pineapple wedge, 3 Luxardo cherries, and paper umbrella

In a 12-ounce glass (such as a pilsner glass), combine the tequila, Aperol, pineapple juice, lime juice, and grenadine. Fill the glass one third full with crushed ice and swizzle (see page 48 for technique) using a swizzle stick or bar spoon. Fill the glass to the rim with additional crushed ice. To garnish, spear the cherries on the umbrella, then stick the point into the pineapple wedge and set inside the glass.

Grenadine

Most people think of grenadine as a neon-red syrup that tastes mostly of sugar. In its classic form, though, it's made with pomegranate juice, which gives complex, tannic notes that marry well with spirits. This recipe will redeem grenadine's reputation.

---

16 ounces pure pomegranate juice

1½ cups Sugar in the Raw
(or any brand of turbinado or demerara sugar)

3 ounces pomegranate molasses (available at specialty stores or online)

Peels of 4 large oranges

In a saucepan over medium heat, combine the pomegranate juice and sugar and stir until the sugar dissolves—do not let the mixture boil. Remove from heat, let cool, and add pomegranate molasses. Twist the orange peels over the surface of the grenadine to express the oils, then discard the peels. Stir to combine and transfer to a nonreactive metal or glass container with a lid. The grenadine will keep in the refrigerator for about a month.

MAKES 3¼ CUPS,
enough for about 60 drinks

KAMEHAMEHA RUM PUNCH

This tiki classic was originally created in 1960 at the Hotel King Kamehameha (since closed) in Kona, Hawaii. I've placed this delicious swizzle on many cocktail menus over the years. It's always a crowd pleaser.

1½ ounces white rum (I recommend Bacardi Heritage)

I teaspoon crème de mûre (I recommend Massenez)

1½ ounces pineapple juice

½ ounce lemon juice

I teaspoon simple syrup

I teaspoon grenadine (page 66)

Crushed ice

I ounce aged Jamaican rum (I recommend Coruba)

Garnish / Pineapple wedge and Luxardo cherry

In a 12-ounce glass (such as a pilsner or hurricane glass), combine the white rum, crème de mûre, pineapple juice, lemon juice, simple syrup, and grenadine. Fill the glass halfway with crushed ice and swizzle (see page 48 for technique) with a swizzle stick or bar spoon. Fill to the rim with additional crushed ice and pour the Jamaican rum over the top. Garnish with the pineapple wedge and cherry.

4

Labor Day

Every year my wife and I pack up the car and head out to my in-laws' place in New Jersey for Labor Day. It is a respite from city life with a big house, expansive outdoor space, lots of trees, and the most gorgeous swimming pool—perfect for those hundred-degree weekends. We don't pack beach towels or sunblock or badminton rackets...there is no room in the car. We pack for battle because we know we are going to be batching cocktails for the masses. We bring booze, garnish, syrups, fresh fruit for juicing, coolers of good ice, and everything else we need to stock the bar.

Over several summers, we've perfected our technique and now we get to spend most of our time in the pool and lounging around. But that first year was a lot of work. So let me go back a bit to the beginning.

My in-laws love to entertain and really bring their A game when it comes to food, atmosphere, and music, but their cocktails needed work, and they knew it. The first Labor Day we spent with them was a year after my wife and I opened Flatiron Lounge, and they were well aware of my cocktail skills. We arrived the day before the festivities and my mother-in-law excitedly showed me to the backyard, where they had a surprise waiting for me. There, next to the glistening pool, lounge chairs, and umbrellas, was a Martha Stewart patio bar—stocked with three different flavored vodkas. I had my work cut out for me. The bar was beautiful, but we had to stock it. So after a trip to the liquor store for some quality spirits, we hit the market for fruit, teas, and sugar and made our way back. Fortunately for everyone, I always travel with bar tools, or a quick trip to the mall would have been in order as well.

We got back and made our syrups, stocked the bar, started freezing ice trays, and created a menu on a chalkboard. The next morning we juiced and cut garnishes, and I was excited to make some fantastic cocktails and enjoy a Labor Day in the sun. It started out innocently enough: a Daiquiri here, a Southside there. But by early afternoon, the backyard had filled up with people and I was making cocktail after cocktail, working a full-blown bar shift with my wife alongside me playing barback, juicing and filling glasses of ice, while the rest of the family and friends lounged lazily in the pool. Not exactly the weekend we'd planned for ourselves, but everyone had a good time, and we eventually got a dinner break.

The following year, we came prepared. I brought the ingredients to make some pitcher drinks in big batches the night before. I printed out a few simple recipes and had them laminated, brought some extra bar tools and basic ingredients, and laid the spread out on the bar. I wanted to be a good host, and didn't want to disappoint anyone who'd attended the previous year, so I made the first round. From there, the guests quickly figured out how to keep their thirst quenched on their own. It was a win-win: I was able to consult on bar technique from my raft in the pool while spending time with my family and friends.

Those summer parties were some of my best work. The recipes from this section are cribbed directly from what I've learned over the past few Labor Days at the pool. They are designed to please your guests while letting you relax a little bit. The key to success is to plan ahead: Have plenty of backup supplies—such as extra citrus juice, garnishes, and ice—to replenish the bar throughout the day. I'd also recommend investing in a few extra sets of bar tools so that your guests don't have to fight over them. Lastly, make sure to stock the drink-making area with a trash can and plenty of bar towels.

Tropical White Sangria

MAKES 30 DRINKS

This sangria recipe was created for the 2005 summer menu at Flatiron Lounge and tested out at my in-laws' house for one of our summer pool parties. Sangria is a fantastic drink for large parties because it tastes better when you make it the night before. The key to a great sangria is to give it time to sit, allowing the flavors to meld together. On a hot day, it is also nice to have a lower-alcohol option, and this sangria can easily be made lighter by diluting it with club soda.

7 very ripe mangoes, peeled, pitted, and roughly diced into 1-inch cubes

10 lemongrass stalks, brittle outer layers removed, cores finely chopped

5 (750-ml) bottles dry medium-bodied white wine

8 ounces Cognac (I recommend Rémy Martin VS)

4 ounces amaretto (I recommend Luxardo)

4 ounces orange curaçao (I recommend Pierre Ferrand Dry)

8 ounces lychee juice

Garnish / 3 pints raspberries

In a large container, mix the mangoes, lemongrass, wine, Cognac, amaretto, orange curaçao, and lychee juice. Refrigerate overnight. Strain the solids the next day and transfer to a pitcher. Garnish the pitcher with a couple of the raspberries.

To make one serving, pour 5 ounces of the mixture into a wineglass filled with ice. Garnish with raspberries.

CUZCO

MAKES 12 TO 15 DRINKS

Pisco, a South American brandy claimed by both Peru and Chile, is an
incredibly floral, fruity spirit—perfect for a hot summer day. To wit, it makes
a great base for a poolside pitcher drink.

20 ounces pisco (I recommend BarSol)

7½ ounces Aperol

¼ ounce kirschwasser (cherry brandy; I recommend
Clear Creek)

7½ ounces grapefruit juice

5 ounces lemon juice

5 ounces simple syrup

Garnish / 3 grapefruits, cut into
slices or peeled into twists

In a 60-ounce pitcher, combine the pisco, Aperol, kirschwasser, grapefruit juice, lemon
juice, and simple syrup. Stir well, then fill the pitcher with ice. To make one serving, pour
5 ounces of the mixture into a wineglass filled with ice and garnish with a grapefruit slice
in the glass or a twist.

DIY BAR SETUP

WHEN THE GOAL IS RELAXATION, a little planning can take the pressure off you while inspiring some creative entertainment for your guests. I organize this setup at my in-laws' house for Labor Day so that guests can make drinks as they please and I can stay in the pool.

There has been an added bonus to this arrangement: Everyone has learned a lot about how to make cocktails. I have received numerous emails over the years from family and friends who attended one of our summer parties and were empowered by the experience to make cocktails at home. These messages were one of the biggest inspirations behind this book, in fact.

This setup should be enough for 50 to 60 drinks. You'll need:

- Two 1-liter bottles of gin (I recommend Gordon's or Bombay dry gin for this occasion, as both are a good value for the price)

- One 1-liter bottle of white rum (I recommend Appleton white)

- One 1-liter bottle of tequila (I recommend Milagro or El Jimador)

- Two 1-liter bottles of club soda

- 3 cups lime juice, in a squeeze bottle

- 2 cups lemon juice, in a squeeze bottle

- 2 cups grapefruit juice, in a squeeze bottle

- 5 cups simple syrup, in a squeeze bottle

- 1 cucumber, sliced into thin wheels

- 4 bunches mint

- Lemon wheels (from 10 lemons)

- Lime wheels (from 10 limes)

- Lots of ice (see pages 8–9 for a guide to ice quantity) in an ice chest or cooler

- Plastic cups

- A jigger (more if you have them)

- A shaker (more if you have them)

- A muddler (more if you have them)

- Bar towels

- Beverage napkins

- Straws

- Trash can (for discarded fruit, ice)

Copy these recipes and laminate them. Set them out at the bar for guests to use.

DAIQUIRI

2 ounces white rum
¾ ounce lime juice
¾ ounce simple syrup

Garnish / LIME WHEEL

Shake the rum, lime juice, and simple syrup with ice until chilled. Strain into a glass and enjoy.

SOUTHSIDE FIZZ: LONDON STYLE

8 mint leaves
2 cucumber wheels
1 ounce simple syrup
2 ounces gin
¾ ounce lime juice
2 ounces club soda

Garnish / CUCUMBER WHEEL AND MINT SPRIG

In the bottom of a shaker, muddle the mint and cucumber with the simple syrup. Add the gin and lime juice and shake with ice until chilled. Strain into a glass filled with ice. Top with the club soda and garnish with the cucumber wheel and mint sprig.

TOM COLLINS

2 ounces gin
¾ ounce lemon juice
¾ ounce simple syrup
2 ounces club soda

Garnish / LEMON WHEEL

Shake the gin, lemon juice, and simple syrup with ice until chilled. Strain into a glass filled with ice, add the club soda, and garnish with the lemon wheel.

PALOMA

2 ounces blanco tequila
1 ounce grapefruit juice
¾ ounce lime juice
¾ ounce simple syrup
1½ ounces club soda

Garnish / LIME WHEEL

Shake the tequila, grapefruit juice, lime juice, and simple syrup with ice. Strain into a Collins glass filled with ice and top with the club soda. Garnish with the lime wheel.

PART TWO

Fall

THE FIRST AUTUMN I SPENT IN NEW YORK CITY WAS INSPIRING.

FROM THE CHILLY NIP IN THE AIR and the gorgeous foliage to the energy of the city when everyone returned from their summer vacations—it drove me to expand my cocktail repertoire with darker spirits, spices, and bitters. I stowed my tropical-fruit-based recipes (I couldn't find quality lychee or pineapple anyway) and started thinking about how I could incorporate fall-friendly flavors like apple, pear, and clove into my bar.

After a few temporary bartending stints around town, I settled behind the bar at a restaurant called C3 in the West Village. When I arrived, it was a typical New York bar—that is to say, the juice came from cans, the soda came from a soda gun, and the most popular drink was a vodka tonic. I was shocked. The bars I'd worked at in San Francisco were all about fresh ingredients; it was the city's status quo. I couldn't believe that New York, the seat of high culture, was so behind the curve. My first task as bar manager at C3 was to cancel the standing order for bottled lemon juice and request cases of fresh lemons instead.

My menu at C3 was a mixture of classic drinks and my own creations—Granny Smith apple infusions, tea-based Martinis, and more. Word got out, and suddenly I was getting visits from people like Dale DeGroff, Audrey Saunders, Ted Haigh, and Tony Abou-Ganim—bartenders who were trying to push the city's cocktail culture forward. They would sit there and quiz me, asking for drinks made with the most obscure alcohol. I had found my people, a small but passionate community of cocktail geeks.

In 2003, along with my wife and a business partner from our San Francisco days, I partnered with a dynamic family of designers and entrepreneurs to create Flatiron Lounge, a cocktail bar located in New York's Flatiron district. The place was packed from day one, always with the most eclectic crowd of locals, tourists, and creative types, all commingling around the twenty-six-foot bar.

The menu built on what I started at C3, with a roster of seasonally inspired creations and a nod to some of my favorite classic drinks. I was behind the bar constantly. We couldn't find bartenders with the level of training we wanted, so I made it a point to give everyone who came through the doors a thorough education (or at least, as thorough as I could, given that I too was still learning) in cocktail history and drink making. I bought every cocktail book I could get my hands on, and my team of bartenders and I would spend hours researching and practicing the proper shake or different variations on the Martini. It was thrilling and exhausting; we felt like pioneers.

When I think back on all the different people who stood behind the bar at Flatiron (and later, at Clover Club), the list reads like a who's who of the bartending world. Many of them have gone on to open their own very successful bars. Nothing pleases me more than visiting a bar run by a Flatiron Lounge alum and recognizing bits and pieces of drinks we might have worked on together.

Many of the recipes in this section are from those early days of exploration and discovery. There are some of the three-ingredient classics that we made so much use of at Flatiron Lounge, drinks like the Manhattan and the Martinez, upon whose shoulders pretty much all other cocktails stand. There are drinks from C3, including my take on an apple Martini (remember when those were all the rage?). And there are Thanksgiving drinks, which I've designed to accompany plateloads of turkey and stuffing—but with enough alcohol in them to help you get through the inevitable family squabbles that come with any major holiday. There are also the drinks that helped me thicken my Hawaiian skin against chilly East Coast wind, ones that come in a mug and warm your very bones.

Fall has always felt more like the beginning of the year to me than January 1: It's when I feel most productive, ready to put my head down and get to work. For that reason, this section is sort of an origin story. Let's start at the beginning.

OPPOSITE:

Martinez

(page 87)

CHAPTER

5

The Classics

As drinkers have become more sophisticated in their cocktail choices, an increasing amount of attention has been focused on the recipes of previous eras. "Pre-Prohibition" is now a term loaded with significance, thanks to a resurgence of classic drinks such as the Old Fashioned and the Sidecar.

Part of the appeal is surely theatrical. Many of these vintage concoctions have elaborate origin stories and evoke an ethos that has been resurrected—think speakeasies, arm garters, and a slew of new spirits made in old styles—for cultish enjoyment.

For me, the appeal is far more basic. These early cocktails are in many ways perfect in their minimalism, and they have become templates for everything that has followed. Basically, they are easy and delicious; they are the drinks that I am most likely to mix for myself at home.

The drink recipes in this chapter are likely familiar to you. These particular versions are not meant to be historically accurate; they are representative of my personal taste. They perform double duty: On a basic level, they are some of the easiest recipes in this book, ideal for pulling out on the fly. On a secondary level, they serve as a cocktail primer. Once you've mastered these, pretty much all other cocktail recipes will make a lot more sense, and you'll start noticing the patterns and pairings that factor into every bar menu.

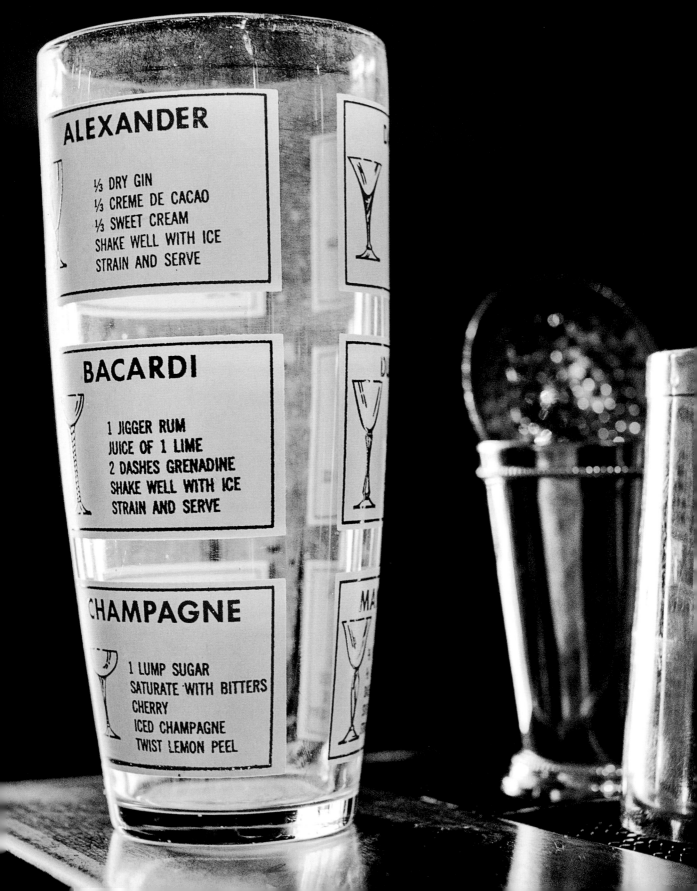

ALEXANDER

⅓ DRY GIN
⅓ CREME DE CACAO
⅓ SWEET CREAM
SHAKE WELL WITH ICE
STRAIN AND SERVE

BACARDI

1 JIGGER RUM
JUICE OF 1 LIME
2 DASHES GRENADINE
SHAKE WELL WITH ICE
STRAIN AND SERVE

CHAMPAGNE

1 LUMP SUGAR
SATURATE WITH BITTERS
CHERRY
ICED CHAMPAGNE
TWIST LEMON PEEL

OLD FASHIONED

Whenever I'm at a new bar and want to get a better understanding of the bartender's style, I order this drink. The mandatory ingredients for an Old Fashioned are few—whiskey, bitters, sugar, water, and citrus—but within that formula there are so many choices to make. Does the bartender use the traditional Angostura bitters, or some other variety? Does she muddle a sugar cube into the glass, or use a simple syrup? What about the citrus: orange or lemon or both? Really, the options are endless, and any bartender worth her salt should use this drink as her calling card.

My version hovers between the old school and the new: I use demerara syrup because I think it creates an ideal consistency while adding depth and flavor. For bitters, I use the classic Angostura, as well as orange. I love Bulleit rye in an Old Fashioned, and I round out the drink with both lemon and orange twists. Also, I'm a big believer that an Old Fashioned needs quite a bit of dilution, so I stir mine with ice for 25 seconds, or until the ice has fallen below the line of the liquid, then pour it over fresh ice cubes, or ideally one large cube, to serve. The size of the ice cubes really does matter for a drink like this. If the cubes are small, stir for less time. More surface area results in faster dilution.

2 ounces rye whiskey (I recommend Bulleit)

1 teaspoon demerara syrup (page 23)

2 dashes Angostura bitters

2 dashes orange bitters (such as Regans' or Fee Brothers)

Garnish / Long lemon twist and long orange twist

In a mixing glass, combine the rye, demerara syrup, and both bitters. Add ice and stir for 20 to 25 seconds, then strain into an Old Fashioned glass filled with fresh ice. Garnish with the lemon and orange twists, expressed over the surface of the glass and rim and dropped into the glass.

OLD FASHIONED MATRIX

Before the word "cocktail" was used as a catchall for any mixed liquor drink, it had a far more limited meaning. It first appeared in print in 1803, and referred to a drink made with whiskey, sugar, bitters, and water (what we now consider an Old Fashioned). Slowly, that formula became more of a rubric, and bartenders began to swap in different spirits and sweeteners. As a result, the original drink needed a new, more specific name, while "cocktail" continued to be used as an umbrella term for this expanding new category.

The Old Fashioned's simple brilliance continues to inspire riffs. Below are a few that I like to make; feel free to come up with your own version.

Step 1

APPLEJACK OLD FASHIONED: In a mixing glass, combine 2 ounces applejack and 1 teaspoon maple syrup.

SCOTCH OLD FASHIONED: In a mixing glass, combine 2 ounces Scotch and 1 teaspoon honey.

AGAVE OLD FASHIONED: In a mixing glass, combine 2 ounces reposado tequila or mezcal and 1 teaspoon agave nectar.

RUM OLD FASHIONED: In a mixing glass, combine 2 ounces rum and 1 teaspoon demerara syrup (page 23).

Step 2

Add 2 dashes Angostura bitters and 2 dashes orange bitters to the mixing glass. Add ice and stir until chilled. Strain into an Old Fashioned glass and garnish with orange and lemon twists.

PRO TIP | *Get creative with your bitters; there are so many great artisanal types on the market now. Try mole bitters with tequila or tiki bitters with a rum Old Fashioned.*

Manhattan

I first started drinking Manhattans while I was cocktail waitressing in San Francisco. Embarrassing confession: I used to add a splash of cherry juice to my glass to temper the strength of the drink—it was my gateway into the world of boozy cocktails. However, it wasn't long before I ditched the cherry juice and fell in love with the unadulterated Manhattan. Now it's probably my single favorite drink. If I could have invented any cocktail in the world, it would have been this one.

My adoration for the Manhattan begins with my love for its base spirit, whiskey. This recipe is a great way to showcase different whiskeys and better understand their various profiles. Start with rye, then make one with bourbon—you'll find a remarkable difference.

The finishing touch is a Luxardo cherry, which you can buy online and in specialty stores. These Italian cherries are the best I've ever had, and in my opinion, house-made versions just can't compete.

---

2 ounces rye or bourbon (I recommend Bulleit rye or Wild Turkey Rare Breed bourbon)

¾ ounce sweet vermouth (I recommend Punt e Mes)

2 healthy dashes Angostura bitters

Garnish / 2 Luxardo cherries

In a mixing glass, combine the whiskey, vermouth, and bitters. Add ice cubes and stir until chilled. Strain into a chilled Nick and Nora glass and garnish with the cherries, speared on a pick.

SIDECAR

This Cognac-based drink was on our first fall menu at Flatiron Lounge. I was astonished by how many people ordered it because someone they once knew (generally a grandparent) had always drunk Sidecars. Rest assured, this drink doesn't need nostalgia to hold it up. As one of the original sours (a family of cocktails that includes the Margarita and the Daiquiri), this cocktail is a crowd pleaser. I'll often make it for a holiday fete because it's one of the few dark-spirit cocktails that almost everyone can enjoy.

Superfine sugar and lemon wedge for rimming

2 ounces VSOP Cognac (I recommend Hennessy VSOP)

I ounce Cointreau

¾ ounce lemon juice

Rim a Martini glass in sugar (see below for technique). In a shaker, combine the Cognac, Cointreau, and lemon juice. Add ice and shake until chilled. Strain into the rimmed glass.

RIMMING YOUR GLASS

Rub a lemon wedge halfway around the rim of a glass to moisten. Place some superfine sugar in a shallow dish and roll the rim of the glass in the sugar—it should adhere to the moistened rim. By rimming only half the glass, you give your guests the option of choosing whether they'd like a sweeter or drier version of the drink.

You can prep your glasses up to two hours before you use them. The sugar will dry onto the rim of the glass, keeping it in place (and out of the laps of your guests).

CHAMPS-ÉLYSÉES

If you really love the Sidecar, you may want to try one of its most famous variations (also a classic), the Champs-Élysées. Green Chartreuse, an herbal liqueur from France, changes the formula remarkably.

2 ounces VSOP Cognac (I recommend Rémy Martin VSOP)

¾ ounce Cointreau

1 teaspoon green Chartreuse

¾ ounce lemon juice

¼ ounce simple syrup

2 dashes Angostura bitters

Garnish / Lemon twist

Shake the Cognac, Cointreau, Chartreuse, lemon juice, simple syrup, and bitters with ice until chilled. Strain into a chilled coupe and garnish with the lemon twist.

MARTINEZ

I was so excited when I first came upon this classic drink, which is thought to be the precursor to the Martini. It's sweeter, thanks to the use of Old Tom gin and maraschino liqueur, but also more complex. There are quite a few Old Tom gins on the market now, but the drink can be just as delicious when made with other styles of gin, such as London dry or genever. This is my favorite recipe for the Martinez, and one that really seems to sit well with the modern palate. You will find that many cocktail bars today serve a predominantly gin-based Martinez using a London dry gin as opposed to the classic equal-parts recipe seen in the past.

1½ ounces gin (I recommend Hayman's Old Tom, Tanqueray Old Tom, Bols Genever, or Tanqueray London Dry)

1 ounce sweet vermouth (I recommend Punt e Mes)

1 teaspoon maraschino liqueur (I recommend Luxardo)

2 dashes Angostura bitters

Garnish / Lemon twist

In a mixing glass, combine the gin, sweet vermouth, maraschino liqueur, and bitters. Add ice and stir until chilled. Strain into a chilled Nick and Nora glass and garnish with the lemon twist.

CHAPTER

6

New York

At C3 in the Washington Square Hotel, I developed a cocktail menu that drew on my experience at the Red Room in San Francisco, my childhood in Hawaii, and my seasonal education in New York. I was a sponge, reading about cocktails wherever I could and trying out new experiments on my own time.

One night, Dale DeGroff showed up at the bar, grinning and full of questions. Somehow he had caught wind of my little program and wanted to see (and drink) for himself. From that point on, my bar became an industry hangout, with locals and out-of-towners in the bartending community making frequent visits. Cocktail culture the way we know it today was in its nascent stages then, almost like an underground movement; we, its members, congregated with enthusiasm.

Our group of cocktail geeks grew, and by the time I opened Flatiron Lounge in 2003, it was clear that the city was drinking differently. The bar was packed from the start and we challenged ourselves to learn on the job, pushing each other to make every drink the best it could be. I'd never worked so hard in my life, but, looking back, I'm impressed by how many of those early drinks still hold up today. I've included a few of them here.

THE SLOPE

This drink is our house Manhattan at Clover Club, and it has been a constant on the menu since we opened. It's also my house Manhattan at home: When friends come over for dinner, this is the cocktail I'll often push into their hands upon arrival. Most of the recipes in this book work with various brands of spirits, but this recipe and Gin Blossom (page 96) were both calibrated very specifically with certain brands. I suggest you try making them as written first before swapping in other bottles.

2½ ounces rye (I recommend Bulleit or Wild Turkey)

¾ ounce Punt e Mes vermouth

¼ ounce Rothman & Winter Orchard Apricot liqueur

2 dashes Angostura bitters

Garnish / 2 Luxardo cherries

In a mixing glass, combine the rye, vermouth, apricot liqueur, and bitters. Fill with ice and stir until chilled. Strain into a chilled Nick and Nora glass and garnish with the cherries on a pick.

C3 Apple Martini

The first version of this drink is very simple, but the flavor is
akin to biting into an apple with a kick.

¼ ounce apple liqueur (I recommend Berentzen)

2 ounces apple-infused vodka (page 92)

I ounce Martinelli's sparkling cider

Garnish / Red apple slice

Rinse a cocktail glass with the apple liqueur: Pour the liqueur into the glass and swirl
to coat; discard any leftover liqueur. In a mixing glass, stir the infused vodka with ice
until chilled, then strain into the rinsed cocktail glass. Top with the sparkling cider and
garnish with the apple slice.

Rinsing

Cocktails, just like food, sometimes call for
a little bit of seasoning. This technique, in
which a glass is coated with a particular spirit
before a cocktail is poured into it, is sort of
like the bartending equivalent of adding salt
to a dish before it's served.

The Sazerac (page 158) is the most famous
classic cocktail that features a rinse. The glass
is coated with absinthe or Herbsaint, and it
creates a truly dynamic flavor.

TO RINSE YOUR GLASS:

1 Add about ¼ ounce of your rinsing
   ingredient to the cocktail glass.

2 Swirl the glass so that the whole interior is
   coated, as if you're flouring a pan.

3 Discard the excess rinse.

If you want to get fancy, you can also produce
a "rinsed" effect with an atomizer, which
produces less waste.

Apple-Infused Vodka

While I was bartending at C3, a customer from Los Angeles told me that the big cocktail on the West Coast was the apple Martini. Intrigued, I tried to make my own version using a Granny Smith apple–infused vodka instead of Pucker. It was a hit and ended up being published in the *New York Times*. I use Granny Smiths because their tartness gives the infusion a nice bite.

8 Granny Smith apples, cut into 1-inch cubes (you can leave the skin on and seeds in)

1 (1-liter) bottle vodka

Place the apples and the vodka in a large nonreactive metal or glass container with a lid and cover. Store in the refrigerator for one week, stirring once a day. Strain the liquid through a fine-mesh sieve into a large bowl, letting the apples drain thoroughly. Discard the apples, funnel the vodka back into its original bottle, and label the bottle. The infusion will keep for three weeks in the refrigerator.

MAKES ABOUT 4 CUPS,
enough for about 16 drinks

METROPOLIS

With the opening of Flatiron Lounge, I made a few edits to my apple Martini invention to make it more…well…Martini-like. I traded the sparkling cider for Pommeau, a French spirit made by combining apple juice with Calvados (apple brandy), and Berentzen Apple Liqueur (a German apple schnapps). This is a fun drink to experiment with. If you can find Pommeau, give it a shot; the liqueur is available online or at specialty liquor stores.

2 ounces apple-infused vodka (page 92)

¾ ounce Pommeau

½ ounce Berentzen Apple Liqueur

Garnish / Apple slice

In a mixing glass, combine the vodka, Pommeau, and apple liqueur. Fill with ice and stir until chilled. Strain into a Martini glass and garnish with the apple slice.

FLATIRON MARTINI

This drink is a great reminder that cocktails should be about what you like to drink, not what someone else deems "correct." I originally made it for a friend who loved vodka, and vodka only. More than ten years later, the recipe reads as a list of what *not* to do in a craft cocktail bar. Flavored vodka and an orange wedge instead of a twist? The horror! Somehow, those things didn't keep it from becoming one of our best-selling drinks at the bar back when I created it. And even though I make it with a twist now, I think it's still pretty damn tasty.

¼ ounce Cointreau

1½ ounces Stoli Ohranj

1½ ounces Lillet Blanc

Garnish / Orange twist

Rinse a cocktail glass with the Cointreau: Pour the Cointreau into the glass and swirl around to coat; discard the excess Cointreau. In a mixing glass, combine the vodka and Lillet. Fill with ice and stir until chilled, then strain into the prepared glass. Garnish with the orange twist.

GIN BLOSSOM

I'm often asked where my inspiration for cocktails originates. A lot of the time, it comes from a certain ingredient or spice, but sometimes it comes from a new spirit. When the Blume Marillen apricot eau-de-vie arrived at my bar, I tried it and immediately knew that it'd make a fascinating addition to a Martini. I had already been using an apricot liqueur in our house Manhattan at Clover Club (The Slope, page 89), so I created this sister drink to serve as our house Martini.

1½ ounces Plymouth gin

1½ ounces Martini bianco vermouth

¾ ounce Blume Marillen apricot eau-de-vie

2 dashes orange bitters

Garnish / Orange twist

In a mixing glass, combine the gin, vermouth, eau-de-vie, and bitters. Fill with ice and stir until chilled. Strain into a chilled Nick and Nora glass and garnish with the orange twist.

PRO TIP

There are many variations of orange bitters on the market. In my bars we use Regans' and Fee Brothers'—one dash of each. Fees' is very light, while Regans' has dominant cardamom flavors. Together they make the perfect orange bitter.

SPICED PEAR

I can never make enough of this drink; anytime I bring it out at a party, it's gone in minutes. The same was true when we had it on the menu at Flatiron Lounge. The infusion took up too much refrigerator space to keep up with the demand!

3 ounces spiced pear vodka (page 99)

½ ounce pear liqueur (preferably Mathilde Poire)

1 ounce pear nectar (I recommend Looza)

Garnish / Pear slice

Shake the vodka, pear liqueur, and pear nectar with ice until chilled. Strain into a cocktail glass and garnish with the pear slice.

Spiced Pear Vodka

10 ripe Bartlett pears, cut into 1-inch cubes (you can leave the skin on and seeds in)

1 (1-liter) bottle vodka (I recommend Ketel One)

25 whole cloves

Place the pears and the vodka in a large nonreactive metal or glass container with a lid and cover. Store in the refrigerator for one week, stirring once a day. Strain the liquid through a fine-mesh sieve into a large bowl, letting the pears drain thoroughly so as not to lose any delicious vodka. Discard the pears. Add the cloves to the vodka and let sit for 20 minutes. Taste the infusion: If it has enough clove spice for you, strain the mixture and discard the cloves; if not, let the mixture sit for 10 or even 20 minutes longer. Once you've strained the vodka, funnel it back into its original bottle for easy storage (but don't forget to label it). The infusion will keep for about three weeks in the refrigerator.

MAKES ABOUT 4 CUPS,
enough for about 11 drinks

Juniperotivo

One thing I love about the bartending community is that it is incredibly generous. Bartenders take care of each other and are quick to support the efforts of their peers. In that vein, one of my favorite parts of our original Flatiron Lounge menus was the "guest" section, where we'd showcase drinks created by talented bartenders at other bars. Not only was it nice for them, but it also opened me and my team up to new techniques and ingredients. This drink, created by Jerri Banks, a talented bartender who was running the cocktail program at a nearby bar when we opened Flatiron Lounge, was my introduction to pomegranate molasses, which is a great cocktail ingredient. You can find it at Middle Eastern markets.

8 mint leaves

¾ ounce simple syrup

2 ounces Junipero gin (or similar high-proof, juniper-forward gin)

1 ounce lime juice

¾ teaspoon pomegranate molasses

Garnish / 1 mint leaf

In the bottom of a shaker, muddle the mint leaves in the simple syrup. Add the gin, lime juice, and pomegranate molasses and shake with ice until chilled. Strain through a fine-mesh sieve into a chilled cocktail glass. Garnish with the mint leaf.

7

Thanksgiving

Thanksgiving is one of my favorite holidays, since it's based around two of my favorite things: family and food.

In my family, the kitchen is the heart of the home. Everyone wants to be a part of the cooking and the many, many tastings along the way before the final version hits the table.

For a bartender, working on holidays comes with the job. It generally didn't bother me—except on Thanksgiving. In the early days of Flatiron I would cling to my right to a turkey dinner by staging the whole thing early. We'd eat at 1 p.m. so I could get to the bar, groggy and stuffed, by 5 p.m. to work.

When I host Thanksgiving at my home, the cocktail game plan always comes down to numbers. If we're a smaller group, I'll generally take requests and mix up different things for different people. If the feast is at full occupancy, I simplify things by setting out a few punches.

If you have a cocktail-savvy group, setting up a station like the one outlined in the "DIY Bar Setup" sidebar in chapter 4 (page 72) is also a great option. Mixing drinks becomes a parlor game of sorts and gives guests something to do while watching football and waiting for the food to come out.

PORT OF CALL

The Port of Call may be the best-selling holiday cocktail of all time at Clover Club. Created by head bartender Tom Macy, this drink not only tastes like fall, but also gives you something to do with all your leftover cranberry sauce from Thanksgiving.

1 ounce gin (Tom recommends a London dry style such as Tanqueray)

1 ounce ruby port (Tom recommends Sandeman)

¾ ounce lemon juice

½ ounce cinnamon syrup (page 55)

1 teaspoon cranberry preserves (or cranberry sauce)

Crushed ice

Garnish / Mint sprig and 1 raspberry

Shake the gin, port, lemon juice, cinnamon syrup, and cranberry preserves with ice until chilled. Strain into a rocks glass filled with crushed ice and garnish with the mint sprig and raspberry.

REVISITING CINNAMON SYRUP

Although cinnamon syrup appears in the "Summer" part of this book, it is equally appropriate in the autumn months. If you have it on hand, it's an instant way to transform a classic cocktail into a decidedly seasonal affair. Using cinnamon syrup in the place of simple syrup in a Daiquiri (page 73) makes it a sweater-weather drink; add it to a French 75 (page 147) for the ultimate sparkler as the temperature transitions.

New York Sour

Thanksgiving is about the main meal, sure. But it's also about all the hours of work leading up to it. At my house, the first cocktail is mixed long before the turkey emerges from the oven. Around noon, I'll set out a cheese plate to hold everyone over until dinner; this cocktail with a slice of funky cheese is one of my favorite pairings of the holiday season.

2 ounces rye whiskey (I recommend Old Overholt)

¾ ounce lemon juice

¼ ounce orange juice

¾ ounce simple syrup

½ ounce medium-bodied red wine

Shake the rye, lemon juice, orange juice, and simple syrup with ice until chilled. Strain into a coupe and top with the wine.

Pro Tip

The red wine should be added delicately to ensure that it floats above the whiskey sour underneath. The tannins in the wine dry out the cocktail with each sip, making for a beautifully layered drink. Measure the wine in your jigger and slowly pour it onto the back of a bar spoon positioned over the surface of the drink to apply it to the top of the cocktail.

LEFTOVER COSMOPOLITAN

For years, the leftover cranberry sauce in our refrigerator would long outlast the leftover mashed potatoes or turkey. Finally I realized that cranberry sauce makes a great cocktail ingredient; since then, it's disappeared quickly. One of my favorite ways to use it is in place of cranberry juice in a classic Cosmopolitan. The sweetness of the preserves can vary, so doctor your drink with a little simple syrup to taste.

1½ ounces citrus vodka (I recommend Absolut Citron)

¾ ounce Cointreau

½ ounce lime juice

¼ to ½ ounce simple syrup (depending on the sweetness of your cranberry sauce)

1 heaping teaspoon cranberry sauce

Garnish / Orange twist

Shake the vodka, Cointreau, lime juice, simple syrup, and cranberry sauce with ice until chilled. Double-strain through a fine-mesh sieve into a Martini glass and garnish with the orange twist.

AMARI

After stuffing my face with way too much food, I generally look to a finger or two of amaro, a classic Italian liqueur made with bitter herbs, to help settle my stomach. This type of spirit has become hugely popular as an industry drink; it's reputed to be a hangover cure and a digestive aid. Amari (the plural of amaro) are meant to be enjoyed neat, at room temperature. Here are a few of my favorites.

AMARO NONINO: Pricier than most other amari, but worth every penny! I mix cocktails with many amari, but this one has so much going on that I prefer to drink it straight.

CYNAR: Very affordable and approachable for someone who is new to digestivos. I particularly enjoy the slightly sweet green-tea notes in Cynar and the fact that it is relatively low in alcohol compared with other amari.

FERNET BRANCA: An amaro that is very popular among bartenders and chefs, Fernet is made up of a secret blend of 27 herbs, including myrrh, linden, galangal, chamomile, cinnamon, saffron, iris, gentian, and bitter orange.

MONTENEGRO: If you've never tried amaro before, Montenegro is a great introduction. Light and gentle, it has notes of orange, honey, rose water, and vanilla, and is one of the more affordable options available.

HARVEST PUNCH

MAKES 10 TO 15 SERVINGS

I never have any trouble falling asleep on the night of Thanksgiving. Between all the cooking, cleaning, and tryptophan, I hit the pillow with ease. But enjoying a mug of this warm rum-and-cider punch certainly doesn't hurt. Serve it after the big meal to help guests relax and digest.

Peel of 1 lemon

3 tablespoons plus 1 teaspoon cane syrup (I recommend Petite Canne, available for purchase online, or make by mixing equal parts cane sugar and hot water)

10 ounces aged rum (I recommend Bacardi 8)

2½ ounces aged Jamaican rum (I recommend Coruba)

10 ounces VS Cognac (I recommend Pierre Ferrand Ambre)

5 ounces Licor 43

10 ounces mulled cider (page 111)

5 ounces lemon juice

5 ounces water

Large ice block (if serving cold)

Garnish / Freshly grated nutmeg (from 4 whole nutmegs); apple wheels (from 1 apple) if serving cold or apple slices (from 1 apple) if serving warm

TO SERVE COLD: Place the lemon peel and cane syrup in a pitcher and gently muddle. Let sit for 30 minutes. Add the rums, Cognac, Licor 43, mulled cider, lemon juice, and water and stir to combine. Refrigerate for one hour before serving. Strain into a punch bowl over the large ice block and garnish the punch bowl with the nutmeg and apple wheels.

TO SERVE WARM: Place the lemon peel and cane syrup in a stockpot and gently muddle. Let sit for 30 minutes. Add the rums, Cognac, Licor 43, mulled cider, lemon juice, and water and heat on the stove over medium heat until hot but not boiling, about 10 minutes. (Do not let it boil.) To make one serving, ladle a few ounces of the punch into a warm mug and garnish with nutmeg and an apple slice.

Mulled Cider

Many stores carry prepackaged mulled cider, which is fine in a pinch. But I like to make my own because the amazing scent permeates the whole house. This cider is great in the Harvest Punch (page 108) and the Brooklyn Buttered Rum (page 115), but you can simplify things by just spiking your mug of cider with an ounce or two of rum.

1 gallon apple cider

20 cinnamon sticks

20 whole cloves

20 whole cardamom pods

20 whole allspice berries

5 star anise pods

4 whole nutmegs

Peels of 2 oranges (no white pith)

¼ cup light brown sugar

Combine all the ingredients in a large saucepan and gently simmer for 45 minutes. Let cool, then strain through a fine-mesh sieve into a large bowl. Transfer to a nonreactive metal or glass container with a lid and chill in the refrigerator before using. The cider will keep in the refrigerator for two weeks.

MAKES I GALLON,

enough for about 40 drinks, fewer if making mocktails

8

Fireside Drinks

In the summer months, our guests congregate toward the front of Clover Club, vying for seats close to the floor-to-ceiling windows that splash sunlight into the room. But from November to March, the heart of the bar moves to the back room, where a blazing fire is always burning in the fireplace. There is something transformative about a live fire: The heat, the crackle, and the scent all contribute to an intimate and immediate coziness.

Hot drinks can have a similar effect, and I learned how important they can be within a few months of moving to New York. One of my first Decembers in the city was particularly cold. On a Saturday, I was out Christmas shopping, and miserable. I ducked into Flatiron Lounge to warm up for a bit, and the bartender on duty made me a hot toddy. It warmed me up in a way that no jacket or scarf could; I slurped it down and went back out, resolute to finish my shopping and get home.

I love to offer hot drinks at fall and winter parties because they're like the liquid equivalent of comfort food. Guests immediately relax and feel at home with a mug of something strong and warm in hand. Additionally, most hot drink recipes are very simple to prepare or can be made ahead of time; set up a station around the stove and let your guests help themselves.

HOT TODDY

The hot toddy is really more of a rubric than a strict recipe. At its most basic, it's a mixture of liquor, hot water, and sugar. While whiskey is traditional, Cognac and rum make equally delicious cocktails; swap in hot tea for water and experiment with different sweeteners.

2 ounces whiskey

1 teaspoon demerara syrup (page 23)

1 dash Angostura bitters

3 ounces boiling water

Garnish / Long lemon peel and 4 cloves

Fill your mug or snifter with some hot water to warm it. To make a long lemon peel, cut the skin in a circular fashion with a peeler, rotating the lemon to get a long enough peel. Pierce the peel with 4 cloves and set aside. Empty the water from your mug. Add the whiskey, demerara syrup, bitters, and boiling water. Garnish with the clove-studded lemon peel.

(CONTINUED)

HOT TODDY MATRIX

Here I've offered four more versions. See which becomes your favorite.

Step 1

RUM TODDY: In a warmed mug or snifter, add 2 ounces aged rum (such as Appleton Estate Reserve), 1 teaspoon cinnamon syrup (page 55), and 3 ounces boiling water.

SPICED TODDY: In a warmed mug or snifter, add 2 ounces chai-infused rum (page 117), 1 teaspoon demerara syrup (page 23), and 3 ounces boiling water.

APPLE TODDY: In a warmed mug or snifter, add 2 ounces Calvados or applejack, 1 teaspoon maple syrup, and 3 ounces hot cinnamon-apple tea.

SCOTCH WHISKEY TODDY: In a warmed mug or snifter, add 2 ounces Scotch whiskey (I recommend a Scotch-style Japanese whiskey like Yamazaki), 1 tablespoon honey, ½ ounce lemon juice, and 3 ounces boiling water.

Step 2

Stir the drink, then garnish with prepared lemon peel studded with cloves
(see page 113) and your choice of a cinnamon stick or grated nutmeg.

BROOKLYN BUTTERED RUM

Buttered rum has a long history in this country (it's thought to date back to the colonial era) and is an institution of the holiday season. This version gets not one but two injections of spice: first through the infused rum, then again with the spiced butter. The resulting mixture is deliciously complex.

2 ounces chai-infused rum (page 117)

3 ounces hot mulled cider (page 111) or boiling water

1 teaspoon spiced butter (recipe follows)

Garnish / Freshly grated nutmeg

In a warm mug, combine the rum and the mulled cider (or water, if using). Add the spiced butter and garnish with nutmeg.

(CONTINUED)

Spiced Butter

Makes about ⅔ cup, enough for about 24 drinks

1 stick unsalted butter, softened

2 tablespoons dark brown sugar

Pinch salt

¼ teaspoon ground cinnamon

¼ teaspoon ground cloves

¼ teaspoon ground nutmeg

¼ teaspoon ground allspice

With an electric mixer or in a stand mixer, cream the butter with the brown sugar, salt, and spices until well combined. Scrape out onto a piece of wax paper and shape into a cylinder. Wrap the butter with the wax paper and store in the refrigerator. Bring to room temperature before making the cocktail. The butter will last for 1 week in the refrigerator or up to 2 months in the freezer.

SERVING HOT DRINKS

As with any other family of drinks, there are some best practices that, if followed, will result in better hot cocktails. When it comes to heating your booze, I've found that darker spirits and wines work best: Red wine, whiskey, Cognac, applejack, aged rum, sherry, and port all make great bases.

The other main consideration is how to turn up the heat. Avoid putting your spirit over direct heat (the alcohol will evaporate, changing the flavor and makeup of your drink). Instead, I suggest heating all of the nonalcoholic ingredients separately, then adding the booze at the last minute, and serving in a warm mug. (Mulled wine is an exception: With a hot wine, just make sure you heat it without bringing it to a full boil.)

Many of the characteristic flavors of hot drinks come from the same baking spices that show up in pies and cookies this time of year: Cloves, cardamom, cinnamon, and allspice all make regular appearances. For the best results, use fresh spices—if they've been on your shelf for longer than three months, it's time to replace them.

Chai-Infused Rum

This infusion can be made two ways. The easy way is to buy a high-quality chai tea and infuse it into a bottle of aged rum for 30 minutes. The alternative, making your own chai mixture to infuse the rum, gives you more control over the final product. It's a key element in the Brooklyn Buttered Rum (page 115) and a great base for a hot toddy (pages 113–114).

2 cinnamon sticks

8 whole cloves

6 whole cardamom pods

5 whole allspice berries

2 teaspoons black peppercorns

2-inch piece of ginger root, cut into thin slices

2 bags Darjeeling tea

1 (1-liter) bottle aged rum (I recommend Bacardi 8 or Ron Zacapa 23)

The spices will release more flavor if you wake them up a little bit. Use the flat side of a chef's knife to smash the cinnamon sticks. Place the cloves, cardamom, allspice, and peppercorns in a mortar and gently smash once or twice.

Place the cinnamon, the smashed spices, the ginger, and the tea bags in a large pitcher. Add the rum and let sit for 90 minutes at room temperature. Strain the mixture through a fine-mesh sieve set over a large bowl, discarding the tea and spices. Funnel the infused rum back into its original bottle and label. The infusion will keep for two weeks in the refrigerator.

MAKES ABOUT 4 CUPS,
enough for about 16 drinks

GLÖGG

MAKES ABOUT 10 SERVINGS

This hot drink, which has Scandinavian roots, is a perfect party beverage.
Just leave a pot of it on the lowest setting on your stovetop and set up a small
garnish station next to the stove. Your guests can ladle their own mugs of
Glögg when they arrive.

---

2 (750-ml) bottles medium-bodied red wine

4 ounces aquavit or vodka (I recommend Linie or Reyka)

1¾ ounces ruby port (I recommend Sandeman)

¾ cup granulated sugar

12 whole cloves

5 cinnamon sticks

4 whole cardamom pods

1 whole nutmeg

Grated zest of 1 orange

Garnish / **¼ cup raisins and ¼ cup slivered almonds**

Place all the ingredients in a large stockpot over medium heat. Bring to a gentle simmer
(do not allow it to reach a full boil), and cook for 30 minutes, stirring occasionally.
Remove from heat and let the mixture cool completely. Transfer to a pitcher or large
container and refrigerate overnight. Strain the mixture through a fine-mesh sieve over a
large bowl, discarding all the solids. To serve, reheat on the stove and ladle into individual
cups. Garnish each cup with a few of the raisins and almonds.

PART THREE

Winter

IT'S NO SECRET THAT I'M NOT A FAN OF THE COLD.

I ABSOLUTELY HATE IT. Every year, around February, when the ground is completely frozen and warm weather is a distant memory, I start my threats (often through various social media channels). I tell anyone who will listen that I'm moving back to Hawaii, or at least somewhere without snow. My friends and family are used to this annual revolt and know not to take me seriously.

Winter's only saving grace is the cluster of holidays that keep me too busy to even consider packing a box. The entire month of December is a whirlwind of parties, packed bars, and presents, and I love the frenzy.

The Thanksgiving dishes have barely been washed and put away when I start making preparations for Repeal Day. Celebrated on December 5, it marks the end of Prohibition and has been adopted by booze slingers around the country as a national holiday. At Clover Club, which takes its inspiration from the days before Prohibition, we throw an elaborate themed party. It has become one of the most popular events of the year and gives me a chance to properly celebrate an era that has played a muse to my career.

The weeks leading up to Christmas are always jam-packed, and this part of the calendar, for all its fun, is a minefield of overconsumption. So I've developed a few tricks for the December marathon, including a heavy reliance on lower-proof drinks. Fortified wines and aperitifs are a lifesaver this time of year; coincidentally, they also pair extremely well with food! For New Year's, I hew to tradition, of course, and stick to Champagne.

January is a quiet month in the liquor industry, so by the time February rolls around, most folks are ready for an excuse to imbibe. Leave it to New Orleans, one of the most important cocktail cities in the world, to provide the pretense: Mardi Gras.

The weather may be awful, but winter is the high season of party throwing. I have learned to love it, even as I grumble with every extra layer I wear, because it provides me with extra opportunities to do what I love most: gather with friends and raise glasses.

| CHAPTER |

9

Repeal Day

To put the rise of the cocktail in context, you have to talk about Prohibition. From 1920 to 1933, the production and consumption of alcohol was illegal in the United States, and that changed the course of cocktail culture forever, so much so that it has become the line by which cocktail history is demarcated—the pre-Prohibition era and the post-Prohibition era.

This book isn't meant to be a history—for that, please read David Wondrich's *Imbibe!* However, Prohibition and the years immediately preceding it have been the lodestar for my generation of bartenders and deserve a bit of contextualizing. When people speak of "classic" cocktails, they are referring to the drinks that were created in the years leading up to Prohibition, the golden age of cocktails. Punches and juleps, sours and slings all came into popular existence during this time.

Just because booze became illegal, however, didn't mean that people stopped drinking. It only meant that, in most cases, the things they drank weren't very good. Cocktails became a way to mask the flavor of inferior bootlegged booze, usually with lots of sugar. With the wellspring of employment opportunity dried up, many bartenders fled to Europe, where spirits were still legal. Harry Craddock was one such bartender, taking up residence at the American Bar at the Savoy in London alongside Ada Coleman, one of the first female bartenders and a pioneer of the industry in her own right. Craddock wrote what is considered one of the first great cocktail books, *The Savoy Cocktail Book*, which included both the American cocktails of pre-Prohibition and the European drinks that he encountered during his time at the Savoy. The recipes still hold up remarkably well and have served as an amazing reference for the industry.

When Prohibition ended on December 5, 1933—Repeal Day—a massive party erupted in the streets. A country full of people who had been drinking in secret was ready to celebrate openly. But the effects of Prohibition were long lasting: An entire generation had come of age during a time when the only spirits available were second-rate. We had turned our backs on a thoroughly American invention—the cocktail—and it would take us decades to rediscover that legacy.

Quite possibly the best thing to come out of Prohibition was that women suddenly became a fixture of bar culture, both as patrons and as employees. Prohibition ushered in the Jazz Age, with most speakeasies featuring live music and dancing. The Jazz Age signified a loosening-up of morals, and the new coed bar scene lent a hand in the debauchery. Women had just been given the right to vote, and they were enjoying some new freedoms—including cocktailing with their men.

As a bartender, I have been hugely influenced by the rise of cocktails that led up to Prohibition, and both Clover Club and Flatiron Lounge are studded with drinks from that time, as relevant and delicious now as they were a century ago. So we make quite an occasion out of Repeal Day, complete with a live jazz band and burlesque dancers. Even if you're not a cocktail history buff, it's a great excuse to throw a party. Plus, Repeal Day falls halfway between Thanksgiving and Christmas, a time most people are not spending with family. In my house, this is the perfect opportunity to celebrate our constitutional right to imbibe with friends.

SCOFFLAW

"Scofflaw" was a name given to people who frequented speakeasies and disagreed with the National Prohibition Act. The cocktail followed shortly after the term was coined, in 1924. This drink is a regular on our Repeal Day menu for obvious reasons.

1½ ounces rye whiskey (I recommend Rittenhouse)

¾ ounce dry vermouth (I recommend Dolin)

¾ ounce lemon juice

½ ounce grenadine (page 66)

2 dashes orange bitters

Garnish / Lemon twist

Shake the rye, vermouth, lemon juice, grenadine, and bitters with ice until chilled. Strain into a chilled coupe glass and garnish with the lemon twist.

A REPEAL DAY FETE

- MUSIC: You'll want a swing-era playlist. Think Duke Ellington and Count Basie.

- WARDROBE: Short flapper dresses for women, and fedoras with classically tailored suits for men (think *Great Gatsby's* Prohibition-era fashion).

- PROPS: Use booze bottles and lots of candles. Filling your bathtub with ice and bottles of Champagne will certainly add to the ambiance and be a nod to the bathtub gin consumed by many Americans during Prohibition.

- GLASSWARE: Scour your local thrift stores and outdoor markets for vintage glassware and cocktail shakers. Often, you will find beautiful glasses for a lot less than if you bought them brand new.

HANKY PANKY

This Martini riff was created by Ada Coleman, the second head bartender at the American Bar at the Savoy in London. I include this classic on the Repeal Day party menu to celebrate women and their new freedom to belly up to the bar.

2 ounces gin (I recommend Tanqueray No. Ten)

1 ounce sweet vermouth (I recommend Carpano Antica Formula)

¼ ounce Fernet Branca

Garnish / Orange twist

In a mixing glass, combine the gin, vermouth, and Fernet. Fill the glass with ice and stir until chilled. Strain into a chilled Nick and Nora glass and garnish with the orange twist.

CLOVER CLUB

My second bar is named for both a cocktail and a place. The cocktail, listed here, is a gin drink for people who hate gin, at turns fruity and dry. In my version, dry vermouth adds a necessary layer of flavor that keeps the raspberry syrup in check. But before the drink, Clover Club was the name of a gentlemen's club based out of the Bellevue-Stratford Hotel in Philadelphia. Founded in 1882, it ran through the 1920s and its membership was made up of the intellectual elite of the time, including many respected journalists and writers. It was the tradition that invited guests—generally celebrities and politicians—would give an address to the club, and each was subjected to the sharp-witted comments of the audience when he finished. These roasts were well documented and word of them spread far and wide.

I find it humorous that the original Clover Club was a real boys' club, and that my Clover Club is run by three women. I like to think we are snarky and bawdy enough to have held our own with those boys.

1½ ounces gin (I recommend Plymouth)

½ ounce dry vermouth (I recommend Dolin)

½ ounce lemon juice

½ ounce raspberry syrup (see berry syrup recipe on page 19; or muddle 5 raspberries in ½ ounce simple syrup)

½ ounce egg white (about half the white of 1 egg)

Garnish / 2 raspberries

In a shaker, combine the gin, vermouth, lemon juice, raspberry syrup, and egg white. Shake without ice for 20 seconds to emulsify the egg white, then add ice and shake until chilled. Strain into a coupe glass, spear the berries on a pick, and lay it across the rim of the glass to garnish.

OLD WORLD PUNCH

MAKES 25 SERVINGS

Punch is the granddaddy of all mixed drinks, and this one hews closely to the original formula, combining elements of strong, weak, sweet, spiced, and sour. Since punch is where the cocktail all began, I always have one on the menu for a Repeal Day party. Additionally, it gives me an opportunity to break out my collection of vintage punch bowls.

Peels of 3 lemons

3 teaspoons granulated sugar

42 ounces Cognac (I recommend Pierre Ferrand 1840)

28 ounces dark rum (I recommend Gosling's Black Seal)

56 ounces brewed English breakfast tea

14 ounces lemon juice

14 ounces demerara syrup (page 23)

Large ice block

Garnish / Lemon wheels (from 1 or 2 lemons) and 1 teaspoon freshly grated nutmeg

In a large nonreactive container with a lid, combine the lemon peels and the sugar and muddle until the sugar looks slightly moistened. Cover and let the mixture sit for at least an hour, or overnight. Add the Cognac, rum, tea, lemon juice, and demerara syrup. Stir, then strain into a punch bowl. Add the ice block and garnish the bowl with the lemon wheels and nutmeg. To serve, ladle a few ounces into a punch cup.

CHERRY SMASH

Born out of my love for brandied cherries, this is a smoking-jacket kind of drink that gets its backbone from Cognac, a popular spirit of the pre-Prohibition era.

2 Luxardo cherries

2 ounces VS Cognac (I recommend Hennessy VS)

¾ ounce orange curaçao (I recommend Pierre Ferrand Dry)

½ ounce Cherry Heering

¾ ounce lemon juice

Garnish / I Luxardo cherry

In the bottom of a shaker, muddle the cherries. Add the Cognac, orange curaçao, Cherry Heering, and lemon juice and shake with ice until chilled. Double-strain through a fine-mesh sieve into a chilled coupe glass and place the cherry on a pick in the glass.

Sherry Sherry Christmas

The weeks leading up to Christmas are so fun, but so exhausting. The bars are packed pretty much every night of the week, and people are drinking more than usual.

After years of experience, I've learned that it's not wise to accept every drink that I'm offered, or my productivity level will rapidly decline. I have to be a bit sneaky about how I drink during December, sticking largely to lower-alcohol drinks. My secret weapon in this deception: sherry, which averages between 15 and 22 percent alcohol by volume but has plenty of complex flavor to anchor a drink.

Sherry is a fortified wine from Spain that comes in a variety of styles, ranging from bone-dry to oxidized and nutty. It has recently become a favorite of craft bartenders because it adds incredible depth to cocktails in concert with other spirits. But I've found that it's equally delicious when operating as the main alcoholic element.

I'm particularly thrilled about sherry's surge in prominence because I've been championing it as a cocktail ingredient for the past decade. Every December since 2006, my bars have hosted the Vinos de Jerez Cocktail Competition: Bartenders from around the country compete to make the best sherry-based drink. It's a celebration of Spain's culture, cuisine, and cocktails, and many of my favorite drinks have come out of the competition's winner's circle.

I've also included port, sherry's darker, sweeter neighbor, in this category of food-friendly, lower-alcohol holiday drinks. Like sherry, port is a form of fortified wine, and it is produced in neighboring Portugal. You typically find it on restaurant menus as an after-dinner drink. Since I prefer an amaro or an Old Fashioned as my after-dinner nightcap, I've learned to use port as a cocktail ingredient that can be enjoyed at any time of day.

Both port and sherry pair nicely with food, so many of the cocktails in this chapter are just as appropriate for a happy hour as they are for Christmas dinner.

DRY SHERRIES

- **FINO:** Pale, straw-colored sherry, dry and delicate. Best served very cold. Tio Pepe is one of my favorites.

- **MANZANILLA:** Pale, straw colored, tangy, and light. Manzanilla is the driest of all the sherries, and can only be produced in the coastal town of Sanlúcar de Barrameda. Best served cool.

- **PALO CORTADO:** A rare variety of Spanish sherry that is halfway between a fino and an amontillado. This light amber sherry is nutty, fresh-tasting, and complex, and best served at cellar temperature.

- **AMONTILLADO:** An aged fino. It is amber in color, and richer and nuttier than fino and manzanilla sherries. Best served slightly cool.

- **OLOROSO:** Full-bodied with rich, raisiny aroma and flavor, but dry. Gold or deep brown in color. Best served at room temperature.

SWEET SHERRIES

- **MEDIUM SHERRY:** Amontillados and light olorosos that have been slightly sweetened. They are light brown in color.

- **LUSTAU EAST INDIA SHERRY:** Oloroso sherry that has been blended with a bit of Pedro Ximénez sherry, giving it a sweet character, best enjoyed chilled. Dark mahogany in color.

- **PEDRO XIMÉNEZ:** Extremely sweet, dark brown, syrupy dessert sherry. The grapes for this style of sherry are picked when they are very mature and are dried in the sun to concentrate their sugars. Older PX sherry will have more acidity than a younger style. Serve slightly chilled.

- **MOSCATEL:** A naturally sweet sherry, produced in a similar way to PX. Moscatel has a floral aroma and tastes of raisins and honey. Serve slightly chilled.

THE BAMBOO

This delicious cocktail was originally created by Louis Eppinger at the Hotel New Grand in Yokohama, Japan. Low in alcohol, this becomes my go-to beverage in December; I am able to imbibe with friends without paying the price for overindulgence the next day.

1½ ounces sherry (I recommend an oloroso or Lustau East India sherry)

1½ ounces dry vermouth

2 dashes orange bitters

1 dash Angostura bitters

Garnish / Lemon twist

In a mixing glass, combine the sherry, vermouth, and bitters. Fill with ice and stir until chilled. Strain into a chilled coupe glass and garnish with the lemon twist.

LA PERLA

This cocktail, created by Jacques Bezuidenhout, was the winner of the very first sherry competition that we hosted at Flatiron Lounge. It was also the beginning of my love affair with the combination of sherry and tequila. Both intensely flavored, these stubborn spirits threaten to overpower each other, but don't. Instead they create lovely balance and depth in the glass.

1½ ounces reposado tequila (preferably Partida)

1½ ounces fino or manzanilla sherry (Jacques recommends Domecq)

¾ ounce pear liqueur (preferably Mathilde Poire)

Garnish / Lemon twist

In a mixing glass, combine the tequila, sherry, and pear liqueur. Fill with ice and stir until chilled. Strain into a chilled Nick and Nora glass and garnish with the lemon twist.

A SPANISH HAPPY HOUR

Spain is one of my favorite places to visit. I love the food, the architecture, the culture, and most of all, the people: They have a real knack for hospitality and go out of their way to make sure you feel welcome. Anyplace that shuts down for naptime in the midafternoon is awesome in my book!

After my first trip to Spain, I wanted to re-create one of my favorite things about the trip: the Spanish happy hour. Spaniards love to snack (as evidenced by the national obsession with tapas), so it's common practice to enjoy an aperitivo alongside a slice of ham or a bowl of almonds in the late afternoon. The La Perla is perfectly suited to this occasion. Invite a few friends over, stir up the cocktail, and serve it alongside a family-style presentation of snacks.

PALO NEGRO

Here's another example of how extraordinary sherry and tequila can be together. This drink, a second-place winner from 2012's competition, was created by Clover Club's own Ivy Mix.

2 ounces reposado tequila (Ivy recommends Partida)

1 ounce palo cortado sherry (Ivy recommends Lustau)

½ ounce blackstrap rum (Ivy recommends Cruzan)

1 teaspoon Grand Marnier

1 teaspoon demerara syrup (page 23)

Garnish / Orange twist

In a mixing glass, combine the tequila, sherry, rum, Grand Marnier, and syrup. Fill the glass with ice and stir until chilled. Strain into a chilled cocktail glass and garnish with the orange twist.

Julie's Sherry Flip

The winter of 2013 was an exceptionally cold one, so I created this flip, which has heavy cream and a whole egg, to fight the blustery temperature. It went over so well that I served it to my family on Christmas Day.

INDIVIDUAL SERVING

3 ounces Lustau East India Solera sherry

1 ounce Ron Zacapa Centenario 23 Años rum

½ ounce heavy cream

½ ounce simple syrup (or cinnamon syrup, page 55)

1 small egg

Garnish / Freshly grated nutmeg

PITCHER

18 ounces Lustau East India Solera sherry

6 ounces Ron Zacapa Centenario 23 Años rum

3 ounces heavy cream

3 ounces simple syrup (or cinnamon syrup, page 55)

5 small eggs

Garnish / Freshly grated nutmeg

TO MAKE AN INDIVIDUAL SERVING: Combine the sherry, rum, cream, syrup, and egg in a shaker and shake without ice to emulsify the egg. You will want to shake for a good 30 to 45 seconds. Add ice to the shaker and shake again, until chilled. Strain into a wineglass over fresh ice and garnish with nutmeg.

TO MAKE A PITCHER (6 DRINKS): Combine the sherry, rum, cream, syrup, and eggs in a blender and blend on high speed to incorporate. Store in the refrigerator until you are ready to serve. To serve, pour 5 to 6 ounces into a wineglass filled with ice and garnish with nutmeg.

RUBY PUNCH

MAKES 8 TO 10 SERVINGS

I'm not sure how port became synonymous with the holidays, but without
fail I receive a bottle of the stuff as a gift at some point during the month of
December. Not that I'm complaining; there are some great ports out there.
This is one of the ways I put these gifts to good use.

Peels of 2 lemons

½ cup superfine sugar

4 ounces lemon juice

16 ounces bourbon, Cognac, or applejack

8 ounces ruby port (I recommend Sandeman)

2 cups water

Large ice block

Garnish / I teaspoon freshly grated nutmeg

In a large nonreactive container with a lid, muddle the lemon peels and the sugar together
until the sugar looks slightly moistened. Cover and let the mixture sit for at least 1 hour,
or overnight.

Muddle the peels again and add the lemon juice, stirring until the sugar has dissolved.
Add the spirit, port, and water and stir again. Keep refrigerated until ready to serve.

Strain the mixture through a fine-mesh sieve into a punch bowl, discarding the lemon
peels. Add the ice block to the punch bowl (or add large ice cubes to individual cups) and
sprinkle nutmeg over the top. To serve, ladle into small cups.

PORT WINE COBBLER

The cobbler was born in the mid-1800s, with the advent of suddenly available ice. It was also among the first cocktails to be sipped through a straw. Loosely defined as a wine-based spirit, sugar, fruit, and crushed ice, the earliest cobblers were most frequently made with sherry. This version, made with ruby port, has appeared on the menus at both Flatiron Lounge and Clover Club. Like the mint julep, it is served on crushed ice, but it is much lower in alcohol, making it an easygoing afternoon cocktail.

1 lemon wedge (⅛ of a lemon)

1 orange wedge (⅛ of an orange)

3 cubes (1-inch) pineapple

¾ ounce orange curaçao (I recommend Pierre Ferrand Dry)

2½ ounces ruby port (I recommend Sandeman)

½ ounce Cognac (I recommend Louis Royer Force 53 VSOP)

Crushed ice

Garnish / Orange half wheel, mint leaf, pineapple slice, and lemon wheel

In the bottom of a shaker, muddle the lemon, orange, and pineapple with the orange curaçao. Add the port and Cognac and shake with ice until chilled. Strain into a Collins glass filled with crushed ice and insert the garnish ingredients into the ice at the top of the glass.

11

New Year's Eve

If you're not careful, New Year's Eve can be the holiday of unrealistically high expectations. The best way to defuse tension and enjoy the night, in my mind, is to celebrate at home, whether with an intimate dinner party or a cocktail party with passed hors d'oeuvres.

Champagne is the customary drink for this holiday, and who am I to argue? In fact, I'm happy to go with tradition, since Champagne is one of my favorite things, both on its own and as an addition to cocktails.

To stretch my Champagne purchase as far as possible, I always make a sparkling punch. A punch also simplifies the serving: Guests can help themselves while I focus on other things, like snacks!

One of my favorite Champagne party cocktails is the French 75. At its most stripped down, this cocktail consists of gin, lemon juice, and sugar, topped with bubbly. But I've hacked it over the years, trying it out with every imaginable spirit and multiple variations of sweetener. You can alter the recipe to meet the vibe you'd like to achieve, or offer multiple versions for guests to mix and match.

Often, my New Year's celebration takes place the next day. After working the big night and sending everyone home safely in cabs, I start thinking about tomorrow's brunch. It's always a very casual afternoon of cocktails, bagels, great movies, and some daydreaming about the year ahead.

FRENCH 75

The French 75 was created in 1915 by Harry MacElhone at Harry's
New York Bar in Paris and published in his book *Harry's ABC of Mixing
Cocktails*. The original recipe listed Calvados rather than gin,
which proves its versatility.

1 ounce gin (I recommend Beefeater)

½ ounce lemon juice

½ ounce simple syrup

2½ ounces Champagne (I recommend Moët & Chandon)

Garnish / Lemon twist

Shake the gin, lemon juice, and simple syrup with ice until chilled. Strain into a flute and
top with the Champagne. Garnish by inserting the twist into the glass.

(CONTINUED)

HER KISSING COUSINS

The French 75 has a formula that works with many spirits, sweeteners, and juices, making it a great party drink. Pick from the below variations, or make a version of your own. (See also the Strawberry French 75 on page 176.)

PISCO: Muddle 1 hulled strawberry in ½ ounce simple syrup in the bottom of a shaker. Add 1 ounce pisco and ½ ounce lemon juice. Shake with ice, double-strain through a fine-mesh sieve into a flute, and top with Champagne.

TEQUILA: Combine 1 ounce blanco tequila, ½ ounce lime juice, and ½ ounce agave syrup in a shaker. Shake with ice, strain into a flute, and top with Champagne.

RUM: Combine 1 ounce aged rum, ½ ounce lime juice, and ½ ounce simple syrup in a shaker. Shake with ice, strain into a flute, and top with Champagne.

BRANDY: Combine 1 ounce brandy, ½ ounce lemon juice, and ½ ounce simple syrup in a shaker. Shake with ice, strain into a flute, and top with Champagne.

BITTER FRENCH (CREATED BY PHIL WARD OF MAYAHUEL IN NEW YORK CITY): Make the classic recipe with the addition of ¼ ounce Campari to the shaker. Garnish with a grapefruit twist.

OPPOSITE:

Brandy 75, Pisco 75, French 75

PIMM'S ROYALE PUNCH

MAKES 10 TO 15 SERVINGS

Who says that Pimm's is a summer liqueur? Add Champagne, and it becomes a party drink for all seasons, as this punch proves. Pimm's was created in the 1840s by an English oyster bar owner, and it became one of the most popular beverages in England. The exact recipe is a secret, but we do know that it is a gin-based liqueur flavored with spices and fruit. It is generally consumed in the Pimm's Cup with ginger ale and a fancy fruit garnish. This festive punch takes it one step farther, letting it macerate with fruit and then adding Champagne rather than soda.

Peels of 2 lemons, plus 2 lemons sliced into wheels

¼ cup granulated sugar

1½ cups thinly sliced cucumber wheels

½ grapefruit, sliced into wheels

1 orange, sliced into wheels

16 ounces Pimm's No. 1

4 ounces orange juice

2 ounces lemon juice

1 (750-ml) bottle Champagne

Large ice block

Garnish / 6 strawberries, hulled and sliced

Place the peels in a glass pitcher or bowl with the sugar (save the lemons for juicing). Muddle the peels until the sugar looks slightly moistened, then cover and let sit for at least 1 hour, or overnight.

Add the lemon wheels, cucumber wheels, grapefruit wheels, orange wheels, Pimm's, orange juice, and lemon juice. Stir until the sugar has completely dissolved and refrigerate for at least 3 hours. You can make this the night before to cut your workload down on New Year's Eve.

When you are ready to serve, transfer the mixture (including the fruit) to a punch bowl and slowly add the Champagne and the ice. Garnish the bowl with the strawberry slices. To serve, ladle into punch glasses.

This punch can also be served Sangria-style in a pitcher and poured over ice.

TOASTING TIP

Before the party, I set aside a tray of clean flutes and store them separately from the rest of the glassware so they're ready to go at midnight for a Champagne toast. That way, nobody is scrambling to find a clean glass as the clock counts down.

THE OLD CUBAN

This is by far the most popular New Year's cocktail I have served in my bars. It was created by Audrey Saunders of Pegu Club back in 2000, and was conceived as a Champagne Mojito. The addition of aged rum and Angostura bitters gives it those holiday spice notes we expect from our winter cocktails, while the Champagne keeps it festive. The Old Cuban is elegant and sophisticated, perfect for any special occasion.

6 mint leaves

¾ ounce lime juice

1 ounce simple syrup

1½ ounces aged rum (Audrey recommends Bacardi 8)

2 dashes Angostura bitters

2 ounces Champagne

Garnish / 1 mint leaf

In the bottom of a shaker, gently muddle the 6 mint leaves with the lime juice and the simple syrup. Add the rum and bitters and fill the glass with ice. Shake well until chilled and double-strain through a fine-mesh sieve into a large coupe or a Martini glass. Top with the Champagne, and lay the remaining mint leaf on the surface of the drink.

NEW YEAR'S DAY BRUNCH

IF YOU'RE ANYTHING LIKE ME, a follow-up cocktail on New Year's Day is a necessity to cure what ails. And for daytime drinking, I crave something light, bright, and refreshing.

Unfortunately, winter is a dark time for fresh produce. Citrus is the saving grace, and blood oranges, which are in season between December and April, provide a shock of color in an otherwise muted drinking landscape. I first discovered the blood orange in 1996 while working at my first bar-managing job in New York City. I put a blood orange Cosmopolitan on my menu that caught the eye of King Cocktail himself, Dale DeGroff. He would later include it in his book *The Craft of the Cocktail*.

Blood oranges grow mainly in the Mediterranean, in southern Italy in particular, but can also come from California. They have a red-orange skin and a sweet-tart berrylike flavor.

Blood Orange Mimosa   *Colletti Royale*

BLOOD ORANGE MIMOSA

Continuing the Champagne theme, this riff on the classic is dead simple but vibrant from the blood orange juice.

4 ounces Champagne
1 ounce blood orange juice

 Garnish / BLOOD ORANGE HALF WHEEL

Pour the Champagne and juice into a flute. To garnish, place the blood orange half wheel on the rim of the glass.

COLLETTI ROYALE

My Italian mother-in-law loves blood oranges, so I named this drink for her. The cocktail is refreshing and bright, and was hugely popular at our New Year's brunch at Clover Club.

1½ ounces reposado tequila (I recommend Don Julio)
½ ounce Cointreau
½ ounce St. Germain elderflower liqueur
½ ounce blood orange juice
½ ounce lime juice
2 dashes orange bitters
1 ounce sparkling rosé wine

Garnish / BLOOD ORANGE WHEEL

Shake the tequila, Cointreau, St. Germain, juices, and bitters with ice until chilled. Strain into a wineglass filled with ice and top with the rosé. To garnish, place the blood orange wheel inside the glass.

BLOOD ORANGE COSMO

This recipe comes from my earliest days in New York, and it still holds up wonderfully, even though Cosmos don't have the same popularity that they did when a certain HBO show was on the air. The Cosmopolitan gets a lot of grief from bartenders today, but it really was the cocktail that sparked the modern mixology movement, and this version was one of the first drinks for which I received attention from the press.

1½ ounces orange vodka (I recommend Stoli Ohranj)
½ ounce Cointreau
½ ounce blood orange juice
½ ounce lime juice

 *Garnish* / BLOOD ORANGE WEDGE

Shake the vodka, Cointreau, and juices with ice until chilled. Strain into a chilled cocktail glass and garnish by placing the blood orange wedge on the rim of the glass.

12

Mardi Gras

Mardi Gras, which occurs each year on the Tuesday before the beginning of Lent, is a welcome signal that the end of winter is near. It also generally falls in February, by which point most people are ready for something to celebrate.

It is a happy coincidence that New Orleans, the home of Mardi Gras, is also a capital of cocktail culture in the United States. Several of the earliest advances in the American cocktail tradition took place in this historic port city. And unlike most places, New Orleans has a knack for preserving history; many of the original bars that figure in cocktail history books are still open and slinging drinks. I made my first trip down to New Orleans in college for Mardi Gras, but began my annual pilgrimage to the city in 2004, when I attended Tales of the Cocktail for the first time. Tales is an annual event that brings together members of the liquor industry from all over the world. Every time I visit, New Orleans has more to teach me about cocktails; it's truly one of my favorite cities in the country.

In this town, it's not unusual to start the day with a cocktail. During Mardi Gras, it's essential to do so! The "season" is beloved by locals and tourists alike and is the epitome of what it means to celebrate. Nobody throws a party like New Orleanians.

I rarely am able to make it down for the main event in person, so I've taken to re-creating the Mardi Gras party at home. I'm not sure whether it's the anticipation of spring, the itch to party, or the spirit of New Orleans, but this gathering tends to be a blowout. With the cocktail recipes in this chapter, plus a little costume flair, you'll achieve the same *bon temps*.

VIEUX CARRÉ

This 1930s New Orleans cocktail is named after the city's French quarter. The drink was created by Walter Bergeron at the Hotel Monteleone, which is still standing and now serves as the headquarters for Tales of the Cocktail, the largest bartending industry event in the country.

1 ounce Cognac (I recommend Pierre Ferrand 1840)

1 ounce rye whiskey (I recommend Wild Turkey)

1 ounce sweet vermouth (I recommend Carpano Antica Formula)

2 dashes Angostura bitters

2 dashes Peychaud's bitters

1 teaspoon Bénédictine

Garnish / Lemon twist

In a mixing glass, combine the Cognac, rye, vermouth, both bitters, and Bénédictine. Fill the glass with ice and stir until chilled. Strain into a double rocks glass over fresh ice and garnish with the lemon twist.

SAZERAC

The Sazerac has a hugely important place in the history of New Orleans and the history of American cocktails at large. It was allegedly the first cocktail to be created and recorded that varied from the original idea of a "cocktail"—what we now know as an Old Fashioned—with the addition of absinthe and Peychaud's bitters. Though the drink was originally made with Cognac, rye whiskey eventually became the standard spirit. Prepare yourself: This drink is serious!

¼ ounce Herbsaint or absinthe

2 ounces rye whiskey (I recommend Rittenhouse)

1 teaspoon simple syrup

6 dashes Peychaud's bitters

2 dashes Angostura bitters

Garnish / Lemon twist

Rinse a rocks glass (see page 90 for technique) with Herbsaint or absinthe by rolling the liquid around the interior of the glass so that it coats the glass's surface. Discard any excess. In a mixing glass, combine the rye, simple syrup, and both bitters. Add ice and stir until chilled. Strain the rye mixture into the coated glass without ice. Squeeze the lemon twist over the cocktail to express its oils. Purists discard the twist, but some people prefer to drop it in the glass as a garnish.

BRANDY CRUSTA

The Brandy Crusta, which was created in 1852 in New Orleans, was meant to be an improvement on the Old Fashioned. The name refers to the sugar crusted around the rim of the glass. The drink is the precursor to the Sidecar (page 84), one of the most popular Cognac cocktails ever created.

I lemon

Superfine sugar, for rimming the glass

2 ounces Cognac (I recommend Louis Royer Force 53 VSOP)

½ ounce maraschino liqueur (I recommend Luxardo)

½ ounce Cointreau

I dash Angostura bitters

Prepare the glass and garnish: With a citrus peeler in one hand and the lemon in the other, start at the top of the lemon and peel on a slight diagonal, turning the lemon, until you get to the bottom. You should have one long peel when you are finished.

Cut the lemon in half, and rub the inside of one half on the rim of a wineglass or coupe to moisten it. Put a few tablespoons of the sugar in a small bowl. Roll the rim of the glass in the sugar. (See page 84 for technique.)

Coil the peel inside the glass so that it lines the interior wall, adding ice to keep it in place.

Prepare the cocktail: With a hand juicer, juice the lemon and strain out the pulp. Add ½ ounce of the juice to a shaker, along with the Cognac, maraschino liqueur, Cointreau, and bitters. Shake with ice until chilled. Strain into the prepared glass.

Hurricane

The Hurricane has a long history in New Orleans, and most recipes for the drink are somewhat complicated, with ten or even more ingredients. Here's a simplified version that is equally strong and delicious as the original. If you are having a big party, you may want to make a large batch of these: The recipe converts well to a pitcher drink and will be drained before you know it.

---

3 ounces dark Jamaican rum (I recommend Coruba)

1½ ounces lemon juice

1½ ounces passion fruit syrup (see tip below)

Crushed ice

Garnish / Orange wheel and Luxardo cherry

In a cocktail shaker, combine the rum, lemon juice, and passion fruit syrup. Add crushed ice and shake until chilled. Strain into a hurricane glass filled with fresh crushed ice and garnish with the orange wheel on the rim of the glass and the cherry set inside the glass.

 **PRO TIP** | *You can make your own passion fruit syrup by combining equal parts passion fruit puree and simple syrup. I also like the syrup sold by a Hawaiian company called Aunty Lilikoi, available for purchase online at auntylilikoi.com.*

TIPS FOR THROWING A MARDI GRAS PARTY

New Orleans is defined by longstanding traditions of exuberant celebration, from the Mardi Gras parades to the Second Lines that take place after funerals. Encourage your guests to get a little rowdy to truly capture the NOLA spirit.

MUSIC: New Orleans is known as much for its music as for its food and drink. Creating a soundtrack for your party is essential! There are quite a few Mardi Gras compilations featuring Dixieland jazz bands or the most famous New Orleans jazz artist of all time, Louis Armstrong.

WARDROBE: In New Orleans, everyone dresses up for the Fat Tuesday festivities. Make your Mardi Gras party a masquerade, asking your guests to wear costumes and masks. You could have a contest for the best costume to encourage your guests to go all out.

PROPS: The official colors of Mardi Gras are purple, green, and gold...not exactly understated. Take the opportunity to make your decorations as over-the-top as you like. Crowns, jester hats, and masks are popular Mardi Gras motifs, and beads are a must.

BARWARE: Stock up on hurricane glasses.

BRACERS & PICKUPS

NEW ORLEANS IS A CITY KNOWN FOR OVERINDULGENCE, so it's no surprise that it has subsequently become known as the birthplace of some of the best hangover cocktails. That said, morning drinks are a storied category: Many nineteenth-century cocktails were designed to be consumed with your breakfast. The following drinks were most likely created for those hurting from their trek down Bourbon Street the night before. Here are three New Orleans classics that I enjoy in the a.m.

JAMAICAN MILK PUNCH

I had my first brandy milk punch at the French 75 Bar in Arnaud's Restaurant in the French Quarter. The following winter, I made this version for a brunch at my sister-in-law's house. She didn't have brandy, so I changed the base spirit to rum and added cinnamon syrup. It is a delicious variation on the classic.

1½ ounces Jamaican rum (I recommend Appleton Estate Reserve)
3 ounces whole milk
¾ ounce cinnamon syrup (page 55) or simple syrup
½ teaspoon pure vanilla extract

Garnish / FRESHLY GRATED NUTMEG

In a shaker, combine the rum, milk, syrup, and vanilla. Add ice and shake until chilled. Strain into punch cups or double rocks glasses filled with ice. Sprinkle nutmeg over the surface of the drink to garnish.

CORPSE REVIVER No. 2

This cocktail was designed to do what its name implies: bring you back from the dead. The corpse reviver was more a class of drinks than one single recipe. They were the hair of the dog, or a little bit of what bit you last night. Corpse revivers came about at the turn of the twentieth century and can be found in many old cocktail books.

1 ounce gin (I recommend Tanqueray or Fords)
1 ounce Cointreau
1 ounce Lillet Blanc
1 ounce lemon juice
½ teaspoon Herbsaint or absinthe

Garnish / 3 LUXARDO CHERRIES

Shake the gin, Cointreau, Lillet Blanc, lemon juice, and Herbsaint or absinthe with ice until chilled. Strain into a cocktail glass and garnish with the cherries on a pick.

Brandy Milk Punch

Corpse Reviver No. 2

BRANDY MILK PUNCH

The milk makes it go down easy, but beware: This is a strong drink. While the classic recipe calls for brandy, whiskey is often used in its place.

2 ounces brandy
3 ounces whole milk
¾ ounce simple syrup
½ teaspoon pure vanilla extract

Garnish / FRESHLY GRATED NUTMEG AND CINNAMON STICK

Shake the brandy, milk, simple syrup, and vanilla extract with ice until chilled. Strain into a brandy snifter or punch cup filled with ice. Garnish with a healthy grating of nutmeg and a cinnamon stick.

PART FOUR

Spring

SPRING IS THE SEASON WHEN I'M READY TO LIGHTEN UP AND CLEANSE MYSELF OF WINTER INDULGENCES.

SOMETIMES THAT MEANS taking a break from booze altogether; other times it means adjusting my cocktail choices to include less sugar and lower alcohol levels. The recipes in the "Brunch" and "Mocktails" chapters in this section are tailored to these scenarios.

That said, these recipes don't skimp on flavor. I'd rather not drink at all than drink something subpar in the name of a diet. The recipes you'll find here are bright, refreshing, and true to my philosophy that the best ingredients show the best results in the glass. Conveniently, they also happen to shine in the context of my favorite springtime meal: brunch!

Two of the best excuses to throw a cocktail party also arrive in spring, and coincidentally they fall right around the same time of year (sometimes even on the same day). Derby Day, which takes place on the first Saturday of May, is a holiday dedicated to celebrating the running of the Kentucky Derby at Churchill Downs in Louisville, Kentucky. It is responsible for the proliferation of the mint julep and a great excuse to wear a large hat.

Cinco de Mayo, which, as the name suggests, takes place on May 5, has become a celebration of Mexican heritage (it is *not*, as many think, Mexico's independence day). Both events are what I like to call single-spirit spotlights—a chance to focus on drinks made with just one category of spirit. In the case of the Derby, it's bourbon; in the case of Cinco de Mayo, it's tequila (or sometimes mezcal, another liquor distilled from agave). Both are great themes for a party, and I like to bring out my favorite bourbon and tequila cocktails for the occasion.

13

Brunch

Back in Hawaii, much of the social activity takes place during the daylight hours. Nightlife is actually a pretty sad story on the island—everyone's too tired from a day at the beach!—so it's common practice to enjoy your cocktails before the sun goes down.

New York's social scene is the reverse, with a high-wattage nightlife that informs the city's rich cocktail culture. The only exception: brunch. New Yorkers are religious about their brunch rituals, including the cocktails that accompany the food. When I opened Clover Club, I knew from the beginning that I wanted to offer brunch, if only because I have a deep love for brunch food.

Daytime cocktails are an entirely different animal from their nighttime brethren. The best ones lift the palate in the presence of a meal and are light and balanced enough that they don't impair you. They can bring you back from the cliff of a terrible hangover without starting you down the same road as the night before.

The cocktails in this chapter are ideal for a variety of daytime drinking affairs, but I've fine-tuned them specifically for that holy weekend tradition of the lazy midday meal. Almost all of them are much lower in alcohol than a typical cocktail. Several rely on vermouths and aperitifs, which have a lower proof, as their core spirits, while others call for smaller volumes of classic spirits.

If you've never hosted a brunch, I highly suggest that you give it a try: It's one of the least stressful types of parties to throw. (You'll be shocked how excited your guests will be with just a bagel and a Bloody Mary.) That said, I have gathered a few pointers in this chapter to make sure your daytime drinking goes off without a hitch.

APEROL SPRITZ

Aperol, an Italian aperitif similar to Campari, is the ultimate brunch spirit. Bright in flavor and in color, it is the ideal balance of sweet and bitter. The classic way to enjoy this beguiling liquor is in a spritz, a cocktail you'll see on every cobblestoned street in Italy. The mixture of Aperol, prosecco, and club soda, garnished with an orange wedge, is dead simple and undeniably delicious.

2 ounces Aperol

3 ounces prosecco

1 ounce club soda

Garnish / Orange slice

Pour the Aperol, prosecco, and club soda into a wineglass filled with ice and stir to incorporate. To garnish, place the orange slice in the drink.

(CONTINUED)

THE SPRITZ MATRIX

Here are three variations on the Aperol Spritz to play with at your next brunch. All would make wonderful pitcher cocktails as well.

CITRUS SPRITZ: Shake 2 ounces Aperol, 1 ounce orange or grapefruit juice, and ¼ ounce lemon juice with ice until chilled. Strain into a Collins glass filled with ice. Top with 2 ounces club soda and place an orange or grapefruit slice in the drink to garnish.

....

COLLINS SPRITZ: Shake 1½ ounces gin or vodka, 1½ ounces Aperol, ¾ ounce lemon juice, and ½ ounce simple syrup with ice until chilled. Strain into a Collins glass filled with ice. Top with 1½ ounces club soda and place a lemon wheel in the drink to garnish.

....

MEXICAN SPRITZ: Shake 1½ ounces blanco tequila, 1½ ounces Aperol, ¾ ounce lime juice, and ½ ounce simple syrup with ice until chilled. Strain into a Collins glass filled with ice. Top with 1½ ounces club soda and place a lime wheel in the drink to garnish.

CLASSICO SPRITZ

If you're serving guests with a love for bitter drinks, consider swapping out their Aperol Spritz for one of these. Gran Classico is a bitter aperitif made in Switzerland based on a recipe from the 1860s. It's an infusion of aromatic plants, including bitter orange peel, wormwood, gentian, and rhubarb.

2 orange slices

1 ounce Gran Classico

1 ounce Punt e Mes vermouth

2 ounces prosecco

Garnish / Orange twist

In the bottom of a shaker, muddle the orange slices in the Gran Classico and Punt e Mes. Add ice and shake until chilled. Double-strain through a fine-mesh sieve into a rocks glass filled with ice and top with the prosecco. Garnish with the orange twist.

VERMOUTHS AND APERITIFS

Vermouth is one of the most important ingredients behind the cocktail bar, but it's also one of the most misunderstood. Essentially a fortified wine infused with botanicals, vermouth comes in a variety of styles (dry, bianco, rouge) and is a crucial element in such classic drinks as the Martini, the Negroni, and the Manhattan. For many years, the vermouth market was incredibly limited. But there has been a recent explosion in vermouth production, with new brands popping up every week that are dedicated to quality ingredients and flavor.

The same is true for the aperitif category. New imports and expanded distribution for classic favorites, such as Campari and Aperol, have made it so that these nuanced spirits are now widely available.

Before you blow your bar budget at your local liquor store, I'd recommend going to your favorite craft cocktail bar and asking the bartender if you can taste a few different vermouths and aperitifs on their own. Once you narrow down which ones you like, it'll be worth investing in those select bottles for home consumption.

I've made a list of a few vermouths that I really like, in order of how much I use them. Oh, and remember, because these are wine-based and have a lower alcohol content than spirits, they should be stored in the refrigerator. I recommend buying vermouth in 375 ml bottles: They take up less space and you'll get through one more quickly. If your vermouth smells or tastes oxidized—characterized by a raisiny, overly saccharine scent—it means that it's too old and should be thrown out.

- **DOLIN DRY VERMOUTH:** Produced in Chambery, France, since 1821, Dolin Dry is light, dry, and clean, and in my opinion makes the perfect 2:1 Martini.

- **VYA EXTRA DRY:** This modern take on vermouth from California is herbal, crisp, and flavorful.

- **MARTINI SWEET VERMOUTH:** Originating in Torino, Italy, Martini Sweet Vermouth is a bargain, and is the perfect sweet vermouth for a Negroni or an Americano Highball.

- **MARTINI BIANCO VERMOUTH:** An aromatic, sweet white vermouth with notes of vanilla and citrus. Try it in the Summer Negroni (page 41) or the Gin Blossom (page 96).

- **PUNT E MES:** An Italian style of vermouth with bitters added that dates back to 1867. My favorite Manhattan is made with Punt e Mes.

- **CARPANO ANTICA FORMULA:** Based on a sweet vermouth recipe from 1786, this bartender favorite is delicious in cocktails or as an aperitif on the rocks.

AMERICANO HIGHBALL

This Italian highball is a classic that gets its edge from the bitterness of Campari. I love it as a brunch drink because it soothes a hangover while cutting through the richness of my favorite brunch dishes, such as Clover Club's pork and grits.

1½ ounces sweet vermouth (I recommend Carpano Antica Formula)

1½ ounces Campari

Club soda

Garnish / Orange twist

Fill a highball glass with ice and add the sweet vermouth and Campari. Top with the club soda and gently stir with a bar spoon. Garnish with the orange twist.

STRAWBERRY FRENCH 75

MAKES 10 DRINKS

Drinks have a tendency to look different in the sunshine, so if
I know that I'm creating a cocktail for a brunch event, I take extra care to
make sure it is beautiful. This is one such drink: It's a showstopper
and will look gorgeous on your table.

---

10 strawberries, hulled

5 ounces simple syrup

10 ounces gin (I recommend Fords or Beefeater 24)

5 ounces chilled lemon juice

1 (750-ml) bottle Champagne or sparkling wine
(for a splurge, I recommend Moët & Chandon)

Garnish / Strawberry slices (from 4 hulled strawberries)
or spiral lemon twists (from 3 lemons)

Place the strawberries and simple syrup in a blender and blend thoroughly. Strain through
a fine-mesh sieve into a pitcher, discarding the solids. Add the gin and lemon juice to the
pitcher, then slowly pour in the Champagne and stir to incorporate. To serve, pour 5 ounces
of the mixture into a chilled flute and garnish with a strawberry slice or lemon twist.

CHAMPAGNE COBBLER

There isn't much to this sparkling drink, but you'd be amazed at the difference between the Champagne Cobbler and a flute of unadulterated bubbly. The oils and simple syrup stretch out the wine's dry notes, while the crushed ice dilutes it into a daytime affair. It's also a visual stunner; if I make one, everyone will immediately request one of their own.

Crushed ice

5 ounces sparkling rosé wine

1 teaspoon simple syrup or berry syrup (page 19)

1 large lemon twist

1 orange twist

Garnish / 2 raspberries and 1 blackberry

Fill a Collins glass halfway with crushed ice. Slowly pour the sparkling wine into the glass. Add the syrup and the lemon and orange twists, and stir with a bar spoon. Fill the rest of the glass with more crushed ice. Loosely place the raspberries and blackberry on the surface of the drink to garnish.

SQUEEZING OUT THE SUGAR

Trying to stay healthy while working in the liquor industry is a real struggle. I'd be lying if I said I never have to worry about watching what I eat and drink. Since sugar is the real culprit in cocktails, I've experimented quite a bit with sugar substitutes. Here's the bad news: I still haven't found anything that even remotely approximates simple syrup. Artificial sweeteners leave a metallic aftertaste and create an unpleasant viscosity. So instead of making a subpar drink with stevia or Sweet'N Low, I've just looked for ways to use less refined sugar where possible. Often, that means using fruit and fruit juice as natural sweeteners, as is the case with these two recipes.

BLACKBERRY COLLINS

The Collins and its variants are naturally low in alcohol, and this blackberry version is frequently my drink of choice when I'm trying to watch what I'm eating and drinking. If you're trying to decrease your sugar intake, consider adding an additional blackberry and cutting the simple syrup back by ¼ ounce.

3 blackberries
½ ounce simple syrup
2 ounces VS Cognac
(I recommend Courvoisier VS)
I teaspoon crème de mûre
(I recommend Massenez)
¾ ounce lemon juice
Club soda

Garnish / LEMON WHEEL AND BLACKBERRY

In the bottom of a shaker, muddle the blackberries in the simple syrup. Add the Cognac, crème de mûre, and lemon juice and shake with ice until chilled. Double-strain through a fine-mesh sieve into a Collins glass filled with ice and fill to the rim with club soda. Garnish with the lemon wheel and blackberry speared on a pick.

JUNIPER BREEZE

This cocktail has no simple syrup whatsoever. Instead, I rely on the natural sugars of the fruit juice and elderflower cordial to give it an inherent sweetness.

2 ounces gin or citrus vodka
(I recommend Plymouth or Absolut Citron)
2 ounces grapefruit juice
I ounce cranberry juice
½ ounce elderflower cordial
(I recommend Belvoir)
½ teaspoon lime juice

Garnish / ORANGE TWIST

Shake the gin or vodka, grapefruit juice, cranberry juice, elderflower cordial, and lime juice with ice until chilled. Strain into a rocks glass filled with ice and garnish with the orange twist.

GREEN GIANT

Judging cocktail competitions has become a part of my routine these days, so you can imagine how many cocktails I taste on a monthly basis. But when I first tried this savory gin drink, now featured on Clover Club's brunch menu, it was unlike any cocktail I had ever experienced. Its creator, Tom Macy, essentially put spring in a glass! The combination of gin, sugar snap peas, and tarragon is magical and impressively savory.

4 sugar snap peas, trimmed and snapped in half

8 to 10 fresh tarragon leaves

¾ ounce simple syrup

2 ounces Old Tom gin (Tom recommends Hayman's)

½ ounce dry vermouth

¾ ounce lemon juice

Crushed ice

Garnish / 1 sugar snap pea

In the bottom of a shaker, muddle the 4 sugar snap peas and the tarragon leaves in the simple syrup. Add the gin, vermouth, and lemon juice and shake with cubed ice. Double-strain through a fine-mesh sieve into a rocks glass filled with crushed ice. To garnish, insert the sugar snap pea, with top pod removed, into the crushed ice.

14

Mocktails

As much as I love booze, I recognize that it is not for everyone. There is a host of reasons why people don't drink. It's always been important to me to create just as special an experience for my teetotaling guests as for those who are imbibing. My bars are, first and foremost, about hospitality, so we strive to create an environment that is comfortable and accommodating to everyone. To that end, we've had a "mocktails" section on our menu at both Flatiron Lounge and Clover Club since day one.

The following recipes go well beyond a cranberry and soda; some of them are just delicious beverages to enjoy at any point in the day while others are meant to actually mimic the flavors of cocktails.

I've relied heavily on these drinks when entertaining friends who are pregnant, and many of them have made appearances at various baby showers that I've been a part of. For the baby shower of our daughter, my wife and I didn't want to deprive our guests of real cocktails, but I mixed in a few of these at the bar so that my wife could also enjoy a drink. They feel far more celebratory than most mocktail offerings, which is particularly appropriate for a baby shower, I think, since the guest of honor isn't drinking.

(And of course, you can always spike these recipes if you see fit.)

ENGLISH BREEZE

Before there were a million specialty liqueurs, I would do what I called "shopping the shelves" for inspiration: I'd go to a handful of gourmet stores to see what kinds of ingredients they had that I'd never tried, and then I'd buy some and experiment with them behind the bar. That's how I came across Belvoir elderflower cordial, essentially an alcohol-free St. Germain. The floral flavor echoes the botanicals frequently found in gins and vermouths. This recipe is the mocktail version of the Juniper Breeze (page 179).

2½ ounces grapefruit juice

1 ounce cranberry juice

½ ounce Belvoir elderflower cordial

1 teaspoon lime juice

Garnish / Grapefruit slice

In a rocks glass filled with ice, combine the grapefruit juice, cranberry juice, elderflower cordial, and lime juice. Roll to mix and garnish with the grapefruit slice.

FIVE SPICE

This drink is the nonalcoholic cousin of a cocktail that appeared on the menu at Flatiron Lounge. Normally I keep my distance from dairy in cocktails, but this drink was too delicious to avoid on principle. It makes an incredibly indulgent morning beverage. If you are very strictly avoiding alcohol, make this drink without the bitters, which have an alcoholic base.
If, on the other hand, you're looking to up the alcohol quotient, adding 1½ ounces of chai-infused rum (page 117) will turn this beverage into an incredible cocktail.

2 ounces brewed chai tea, sweetened and chilled

1½ ounces whole milk

1 teaspoon grade B maple syrup

½ teaspoon pure vanilla extract

2 dashes Angostura bitters

White of 1 small egg

Garnish / Freshly grated nutmeg

In a shaker, combine the tea, milk, maple syrup, vanilla extract, bitters, and egg white. Shake without ice for 30 seconds to emulsify the egg white. Add ice and shake well to chill, then strain into a chilled coupe and garnish with nutmeg.

FAUX 75

So many first-time moms tell me that the thing they missed most about cocktails during pregnancy was the bitter flavors in various drinks. With this recipe, I've tried to trick the mind into thinking that it's the real thing by using a bitter lemon soda.

---

1 ounce lemon juice

1 ounce simple syrup

Fever Tree Bitter Lemon soda

Garnish / Lemon twist

Shake the lemon juice and simple syrup with ice until chilled. Strain into a flute and top with a few ounces of the soda. Garnish with the lemon twist.

LYCHEE & LEMONGRASS FIZZ

This mocktail version of Leilani's Fizz (page 63) conjures up an island escape. If you've already made the lemongrass syrup, it's a cinch to pull together.

2 fresh or canned lychee nuts

3 ounces lychee juice

½ ounce lime juice

½ ounce lemongrass syrup (page 62)

Soda water

Garnish / Lemongrass stalk (8 to 10 inches long) and lime wheel

In the bottom of a shaker, muddle the lychees. Add the lychee juice, lime juice, and lemongrass syrup and shake with ice. Double-strain through a fine-mesh sieve into a highball glass filled with ice. Top with soda water and garnish with the lemongrass stalk and lime wheel.

KEEP YOUR DRINKS STRAIGHT

If you serve both alcoholic and nonalcoholic versions of the same drink at an event, make sure to garnish them differently or serve them in different glasses, so that the boozy drinks don't end up in the wrong hands.

Juniper & Tonic

The juniper syrup, made with juniper berries, is the main flavoring agent here, and it echoes the piney, herbal, and citrus notes of a classic G&T.

---

1 ounce juniper syrup (page 189)

¾ ounce lime juice

Ice

High-quality tonic water (I recommend Canada Dry or Seagram's)

Garnish / Lime wheel

Shake the juniper syrup and the lime juice with ice until chilled. Strain into an ice-filled double rocks glass. Fill to the rim with the tonic water and garnish with the lime wheel.

Juniper Syrup

This syrup isn't as versatile as some of the others in this book,
but it keeps for quite a while in the refrigerator.

---

3 tablespoons juniper berries (available from specialty spice markets and online)

Peel of 1 orange

3 cardamom pods

1 cup water

1 cup granulated sugar

In a saucepan, muddle the juniper berries until all have broken open. Add the orange peel, cardamom pods, and water and cook over medium heat until the mixture simmers. Add the sugar and keep at a simmer for 20 minutes. Transfer the mixture to a heatproof container, cover, and let sit in the refrigerator overnight. Strain it through a fine-mesh sieve into a nonreactive metal or glass container with a lid. The syrup can be stored in the refrigerator for up to one month.

MAKES 13 OUNCES,
enough for about 13 drinks

LILIKOI

My childhood home in Hawaii had a mango tree in the backyard, and we were always scrambling to come up with new ways to use the fruit. Inevitably it would end up in the blender, as Margaritas for my parents and smoothies for me. One of my chores was to rake up the leaves from under the tree, and on the day of my junior prom, some of the sap from the tree fell on my shoulder as I was raking. I must have had an allergic reaction, because in all the pictures of me in my prom dress, my shoulder is red and splotchy. But even that embarrassment couldn't quell my love of mangoes; this drink is an ode to the mango smoothies of my youth.

2 ounces mango and passion fruit puree (recipe follows)

1 ounce passion fruit juice

½ ounce lime juice

½ ounce lemon juice

½ ounce simple syrup

Garnish / Orchid

Shake the puree, juices, and simple syrup with ice until chilled. Strain into a hurricane glass. Garnish with an orchid.

Mango & Passion Fruit Puree

Makes 11 ounces, enough for about 11 drinks

1 ripe mango, peeled, pitted, and roughly diced into 1-inch pieces

3 ounces passion fruit juice

Combine the mango and passion fruit juice in a blender and blend on high speed until smooth. Transfer to a nonreactive metal or glass container with a lid and refrigerate until ready to use. It will keep for one week in the refrigerator.

CUCUMBER-MINT COOLER

Cucumber is a great addition to a mocktail, because its clean vegetal flavor mimics some of the botanicals frequently found in gin. This drink is unbelievably refreshing, like the best spa water you've ever had.

2 wheels English cucumber

10 mint leaves

2 ounces simple syrup

1¼ ounces lime juice

Club soda

Garnish / Cucumber slice and mint sprig

In a shaker, muddle the cucumber wheels and mint leaves with the simple syrup until the cucumbers have expressed their juices. Add the lime juice and shake with ice until chilled. Strain into a wineglass filled with ice. Top with a splash of club soda and garnish with the cucumber slice and mint sprig laid on the surface of the drink.

LUCKY CLOVER

We wanted to create a nonalcoholic version of Clover Club's namesake cocktail, so we came up with this bright and tart offering. The orange-flower water, available online and in specialty stores, is an amazing mocktail ingredient, and adds a depth of flavor that always leaves drinkers guessing.

2 ounces lemon juice

2 ounces raspberry syrup (see berry syrup recipe on page 19;
or muddle 4 raspberries in 2 ounces simple syrup)

4 dashes orange-flower water

¾ ounce egg white

2 ounces soda water

Garnish / 3 raspberries

In a shaker, combine the lemon juice, syrup, orange-flower water, and egg white. Shake well without ice for 20 seconds to emulsify the egg white. Add ice and shake again until chilled. Strain into a chilled wineglass, top with soda water, spear the berries on a pick, and lay it across the rim of the glass to garnish.

15

Cinco de Mayo

I know that spring has arrived when I switch from stiff bourbon drinks to bright tequila drinks. Conveniently, the switchover occurs right around Cinco de Mayo, so I throw a party each year to officially kick off the season.

Everyone has a tequila story. Most of the time, it involves one really bad night in college followed by a period of tequila abstinence. I'm as guilty as anyone: I have known shots of Montezuma and I've known its revenge.

Unfortunately, there is a reason that we all have those stories: Tequila is irresistibly fun and encourages overindulgence. A bottle of tequila among friends is the fastest way to create a party. Therefore, it's one of my favorite spirits to use in cocktails when I'm entertaining. But tequila is more than just a party trick. Made only in the Mexican state of Jalisco, it's one of the most complex spirits in existence, and, at its best, it's the product of lots of craftsmanship and patience. Like vodka, however, tequila is at the center of a major marketing complex that tends to prioritize glitz over quality. So when shopping for tequila, look for bottles that are distilled from 100 percent agave.

The drinks in this chapter capitalize on the festive nature of this Mexican import, but they're a far cry from the shots of your youth. From a simple, sophisticated Margarita to a ruby-red beet cocktail, these recipes will introduce you and your guests to a different side of tequila.

TOMMY'S MARGARITA

Julio Bermejo, the co-owner of Tommy's Mexican Restaurant in San Francisco, makes his famous Margarita with agave nectar in place of triple sec. Julio's recipe really showcases the delicious tequila and brings the calorie count down at the same time. Double win.

I lime wedge

2 ounces reposado tequila

I ounce lime juice

½ ounce agave nectar

Prepare a rocks glass by moistening the rim with the lime wedge and dipping the rim into kosher salt (see page 84 for technique). Reserve the lime wedge for garnishing. Fill the glass with ice. In a shaker, combine the tequila, lime juice, and agave nectar. Add ice and shake until chilled. Strain into the prepared glass and garnish with the lime wedge.

SIESTA

Former Flatiron Lounge and Clover Club bartender Katie Stipe created this cocktail, and it is pretty much universally loved by those who try it. I consider this a modern classic in its own right—this drink has appeared on bar menus across the country.

1½ ounces blanco tequila (Katie recommends Ocho)

¼ ounce Campari

¾ ounce lime juice

½ ounce grapefruit juice

¾ ounce simple syrup

Garnish / Lime wheel

Shake the tequila, Campari, lime juice, grapefruit juice, and simple syrup with ice until chilled. Strain into a chilled cocktail glass and place the lime wheel on the rim of the glass to garnish.

We Got the Beet

Be forewarned: This recipe is a little involved. That being said, I love making it for parties because the dramatic color and unique flavor always impress my guests. This cocktail came about as a collaboration with our chef at Clover Club; he made the shrub and I made the syrup. Both were so delicious and intriguing that the cocktail came together in a flash.

1½ ounces blanco tequila (I recommend Pueblo Viejo or El Tesoro)

½ ounce mezcal (I recommend Del Maguey Vida)

¾ ounce lime juice

½ ounce beet shrub (recipe follows)

½ ounce beet syrup (recipe follows)

Garnish / 2 slices yellow beet or 2 lime wheels

Shake the tequila, mezcal, lime juice, shrub, and syrup with ice until chilled. Strain into a rocks glass filled with ice. To garnish, lay the yellow beet slices or lime wheels on the surface of the drink.

(CONTINUED)

Beet Shrub

Makes 3¾ cups, enough for about 15 drinks

Shrub is an old form of drinking vinegar that has recently made something
of a comeback. Vinegar is a wonderful agent of acidity and works
just as well in drinks as it does in food. You can mix this shrub with club
soda to make a natural, grown-up soda pop. Look for fresh beet juice in
natural food stores or at juice bars.

8 ounces fresh beet juice

2 cups granulated sugar

10 ounces sherry vinegar

4 cinnamon sticks

In a medium saucepan over medium heat, combine the beet juice, sugar,
vinegar, and cinnamon sticks. Bring to a simmer, stirring, and cook until
the sugar dissolves. Remove from heat and let stand for 15 minutes, then
strain the mixture through a fine-mesh sieve set over a bowl. Transfer the
shrub to a nonreactive metal or glass container with a lid and store in the
refrigerator until ready to use. It will keep in the refrigerator for 1 week.

Beet Syrup

Makes 1½ cups, enough for about 24 drinks

Beets are a unique source of sugar and this syrup has a deliciously earthy quality that I really love. Its striking color is lovely in the glass, but be sure to wear an apron while you prepare this—it stains like crazy!

15 mint leaves

2 large beets, tops removed, peeled and cubed

1 (3-inch) chunk ginger root, cleaned and cut into small pieces

1 cup granulated sugar

½ cup water

In a medium saucepan over medium heat, combine the mint, beets, ginger, sugar, and water. Bring to a simmer and reduce heat to low; stirring occasionally, cook for another 15 minutes. Remove the mixture from heat and let it cool completely. Strain the syrup through a fine-mesh sieve into a nonreactive metal or glass container with a lid and store in the refrigerator until ready to use. It will last in the refrigerator for up to one week.

UNCLE BUCK

Brad Farran, one of our former head bartenders at Clover Club, came up with this buck (a family of refreshing ginger drinks), and it quickly became a favorite of mine. The interplay between the herbal nature of the Chartreuse and the bright zippy notes of tequila and pineapple is magical and unexpected.

---

2 ounces blanco tequila (Brad recommends Milagro Silver)

¼ ounce green Chartreuse

1 ounce pineapple juice

¾ ounce lime juice

½ ounce ginger syrup (page 33)

Garnish / Pineapple slice

Shake the tequila, Chartreuse, pineapple juice, lime juice, and ginger syrup with ice until chilled. Strain into a Collins glass filled with ice. Garnish with the pineapple slice inside the glass.

SUEY'S SANGRITA

MAKES 5 DRINKS

Here's the thing about shots: They invite bad behavior and overconsumption (just take a peek at any college bar to see what I mean), but they are also kind of fun. In this cocktail, the tequila is served on the side as a shot, but the Sangrita keeps things in check. I cribbed the recipe from my wife, Sue, who loves all tomato-based drinks. Some people like to sip the tequila separately from the cocktail, but I like to pour my shot right into the glass and enjoy it like a Bloody Mary. I promise that your guests will flock to try out this interactive combo.

I jalapeño, sliced in half and seeded (leave the seeds in for a spicier Sangrita)

15 ounces tomato juice

6 ounces orange juice

2 ounces grapefruit juice

I ounce lime juice

I ounce Tabasco hot sauce

½ ounce Cholula hot sauce

I teaspoon salt

Pinch smoked paprika

Pinch white pepper

10 ounces blanco tequila (I recommend Partida Blanco)

In a pitcher, combine the jalapeño, juices, Tabasco, Cholula, salt, paprika, and pepper. Stir, cover, and let the mixture sit in the refrigerator for 30 minutes. Remove the jalapeño. To serve, pour 5 ounces of the Sangrita into a Collins glass filled with ice and serve alongside a 2-ounce shot of blanco tequila.

ROSARITO BEACH COLLINS

Any time I pair tequila with watermelon, the crowds come running. This cocktail would make an excellent large-format drink, too; if you go that route, consider serving the punch in a hollowed-out watermelon half.

4 cubes (1-inch) watermelon

2 cucumber wheels

½ ounce grenadine (page 66)

2 ounces blanco tequila (I recommend Pueblo Viejo Blanco)

3 dashes absinthe (I recommend Pernod)

¾ ounce lime juice

Pinch salt

1 ounce club soda

Garnish / Watermelon balls and cucumber wheels on a skewer

In the bottom of a shaker, muddle the watermelon and cucumber wheels with the grenadine. Add the tequila, absinthe, lime juice, and salt and shake with ice until chilled. Double-strain through a fine-mesh sieve into a Collins glass filled with ice. Top with the club soda and place the melon-and-cucumber skewer in the glass to garnish.

CHAPTER

16

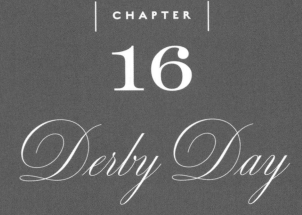

Derby Day

I wasn't really clued in to the Kentucky Derby until I moved to New York. A friend brought me to my first Derby party, complete with giant hats, mint juleps, cigars, and betting, and I was hooked!

Much of my love for this Southern institution stems from my love for the mint julep. The classic drink is simple; so simple, in fact, that it can be easy to mess up. Each component—bourbon, mint, sugar, and ice—must be handled carefully to ensure the most delicious drink possible.

In addition to my classic julep recipe, this section includes a few like-minded drinks that we developed as part of a Derby-themed flight at Flatiron Lounge.

MINT

The freshness and quality of your mint are crucial to a proper mint julep. Don't buy your mint more than twenty-four hours before your party, and try to purchase it from the farmers' market if possible. Avoid using the mint in those little plastic containers, which is generally several days old and already beginning to wilt by the time it hits the shelves.

Generally I buy double the mint I need for a recipe: I pick the leaves of half the mint (for muddling) and trim the other half into sprigs for garnish.

Mint wilts quickly if left out; storing it properly will keep it fresh and vibrant and will largely improve the quality of your julep. To store your mint, wrap it in a damp (but not wet) paper towel and place it in a Ziploc bag in the refrigerator. You will want to wait until you are ready to make your cocktails to pick your muddling mint and make your sprigs. To store mint sprigs for garnishing during your party, trim the bottoms of the stems, then place the sprigs upside down (stem facing up, like a backward bouquet) in a double rocks glass and fill loosely with crushed ice and water so the mint leaves are submerged. Storing them this way will give you picture-perfect juleps with lovely bouquets of mint!

BOURBON

There are so many different styles of bourbon to choose from. A bourbon whiskey with more rye in its makeup will produce a spicier julep, while one made with a majority of wheat or corn will create a sweeter julep. I generally look to higher-proof bourbon, something over 45 percent ABV (90 proof) to stand up to the water. Here are some of my favorite bourbons for this iconic drink:

- BULLEIT

- BUFFALO TRACE

- WILD TURKEY RARE BREED

- MAKER'S MARK

- BLANTON'S

Classic Mint Julep

This classic beverage is a mini-evolution in a glass. The drink is at its strongest in the beginning, before the ice has had a chance to melt. There is a sweet spot about ten minutes after the drink is made where the dilution is *perfect*. And by the time you reach the end, the bourbon has been watered down to a deliciously refreshing slushy.

Aromatics are essential to the julep-drinking experience. I garnish each julep with a few huge mint sprigs placed right next to the straw so that my guests get a burst of that delicious smell with every sip.

8 to 10 mint leaves

½ ounce demerara syrup (page 23)

2 ounces bourbon (choose from my list of favorites on page 207)

Crushed ice

Garnish / 3 mint sprigs

In a chilled julep cup or rocks glass, muddle the mint with the demerara syrup. Add the bourbon and fill the glass halfway with crushed ice. Swizzle with a bar spoon. Top with more ice and swizzle until there is a frost on the outside of the cup. Garnish with the mint sprigs.

BOURBON SMASH

This cocktail, popularized by Dale DeGroff, is the godfather of muddled drinks and a natural forebear of creations like the Caipirinha and the Mojito. By muddling pieces of lemon, you get the flavor of both the juice and the essential oils in the peels, which add an impressive layer of complexity.

3 lemon wedges

5 mint leaves

¾ ounce simple syrup

2 ounces bourbon (choose from my list of favorites on page 207)

Garnish / Mint sprig

In the bottom of a shaker, muddle the lemon wedges and mint with the simple syrup. Add the bourbon and shake with ice until chilled. Double-strain through a fine-mesh sieve into a rocks glass filled with ice. Garnish with the mint sprig.

Sweet Tea Julep

This version of the julep uses mint tea syrup instead of fresh mint. It's a great option if you're hosting a large crowd, since there's no muddling involved and you can make the syrup ahead of time.

2 ounces bourbon (choose from my list of favorites on page 207)

½ ounce mint tea simple syrup (page 53)

Crushed ice

Garnish / Three mint sprigs

Combine the bourbon and syrup in a chilled julep cup. Fill halfway with crushed ice and swizzle with a bar spoon. Top with more ice and swizzle until there is a frost on the outside of the cup. Garnish with the mint sprigs.

MASON JAR

I've learned to rely on jams and preserves when I don't have more fresh ingredients (such as stone fruit) on hand. And since the South is all about pickling and preserving, relying on these put-ups seems an appropriate homage to the home of the Derby. You can absolutely swap out the apricot jam for another type; orange marmalade, berry jam, or plum preserves would all make delicious variations.

1½ ounces bourbon (choose from my list of favorites on page 207)

1 ounce Lillet Blanc

½ ounce lemon juice

½ ounce orange juice

Heaping teaspoon apricot preserves

Garnish / Orange slice

Shake the bourbon, Lillet, lemon juice, orange juice, and apricot preserves with ice until chilled. Strain into a Mason jar or rocks glass filled with ice and garnish with the orange slice on the top of the drink.

MINT JULES

It's a general rule that you mix lemon juice with brown spirits and lime juice with clear spirits. But rules are meant to be broken, and I've done so here with delicious results.

3 lime wedges

10 mint leaves

2½ ounces bourbon (choose from my list of favorites on page 207)

¾ ounce simple syrup

Splash of soda water

Garnish / 1 mint leaf

In the bottom of a shaker, muddle the lime wedges until you have expressed the juice and oils. Add the 10 mint leaves and gently muddle a little bit more. Add the bourbon and syrup and shake with ice. Double-strain through a fine-mesh sieve into a chilled cocktail glass and top with the soda water. Lay the remaining mint leaf on the surface of the drink to garnish.

Southern Peach

If you're in need of an alternative to mint, this drink is a great way to go.
Peaches can be overwhelmingly sweet, so it takes a strong, boozy spirit like
bourbon to keep them in check. The sparkling wine lightens it up enough
to warrant afternoon drinking. If you choose to muddle fresh peach,
you may need to increase the volume of simple syrup, since the sweetness
of peaches varies.

1 ounce bourbon (choose from my list of favorites on page 207)

½ ounce peach nectar (or ½ peach, muddled)

¼ ounce lemon juice

¼ ounce simple syrup

Sparkling wine

Garnish / 3 peach slices

Shake the bourbon, peach nectar, lemon juice, and simple syrup with ice until chilled.
Double-strain into a chilled flute and fill to the top with sparkling wine. Garnish with a
speared fan of peach slices.

ACKNOWLEDGMENTS

There are so many people to thank

FOR MAKING THIS BOOK HAPPEN.

My agent, Jonah Straus, for his continued support and good advice. Thank you for giving me the push I needed to take on this project.

Kaitlyn Goalen for all of her hard work on the book, and for keeping me organized and on track!

Karen Murgolo and the team at Grand Central Publishing, including Kallie Shimek, Laura Cherkas, Elizabeth Connor, Nick Small, Morgan Hedden, and our wonderful designer, Laura Palese.

Daniel Krieger for his beautiful photos, and for making the shoots fun. Toby Cecchini for loaning us the Long Island Bar for one of our photo shoots, and Jessica Wohlers for her assistance with styling on the Red Hook shoot.

My partners at Clover Club, Christine Williams, Susan Fedroff, and Tom Macy, for making this possible and for giving me the time to work on this book. I am so thankful to have such inspiring, hardworking partners.

The many bartenders I have worked with over the years who contributed their fantastic recipes to this book, including Tom Macy, Brad Farran, Audrey Saunders, Ivy Mix, Katie Stipe, Phil Ward, Brian Miller, Julio Bermejo, Jerri Banks, and Jacques Bezuidenhout.

My friends and mentors who invited me to be a part of their cocktail family and showed me that there were others out there who cared about putting something of quality in a glass: Dale DeGroff, David Wondrich, Tony Abou-Ganim, Audrey Saunders, Charlotte Voisey, Andy Seymour, Simon Ford, and Steve Olson.

My parents and siblings Sue, Rick, Chris, and Jennifer for their support, and for the revolving door of house guests we always had, which taught me the art of entertaining.

Finally, my wife, Susan, and my daughter, Maya, for putting up with me while I wrote this book. I love you both so much! Susan, none of this is possible without you...and it certainly wouldn't be as much fun.

Sources

AMAZON.COM
The best source for Petite Canne Sugar Cane Syrup.

AUNTYLILIKOI.COM
My choice for Hawaiian passion fruit syrup.

BUFFALOTRACE.COM
Sells both Peychaud's Bitters and Regans' Orange Bitters.

COCKTAILKINGDOM.COM
One-stop shopping for quality barware, glassware, and cocktail books. Cocktail Kingdom also stocks some hard-to-find bitters and syrups.

CRATEANDBARREL.COM
Offers a wide range of affordable glassware perfect for home use.

GOURMETFOODSTORE.COM
Sells passion fruit puree.

INPURSUITOFTEA.COM
Sebastian Beckwith travels the world in search of the best tea and sells it through this site. I have used his teas in many cocktails over the years.

JULIEREINER.COM
Offers glassware, bar tools, and Clover Club syrups all geared toward the home bartender.

KALUSTYANS.COM
This Manhattan shop is a cocktail bartender's friend. They stock a wide variety of bitters, sugars, spices, purees, and syrups.

ORGEATWORKS.COM
Sells toasted almond and macadamia nut orgeat syrup.

ORIENTALTRADING.COM
Sells themed party supplies including tiki, Fourth of July, and Christmas decorations.

PACIFIKOOL.COM
Sells some of the best ginger syrup on the market, made from ginger grown exclusively in Hawaii.

RETROPLANET.COM
Sells tiki and retro party supplies.

SERENDIPITEA.COM
Sells great teas for infusing into spirits. I highly recommend the Lili'uokalani Chinese black tea for use in the Hawaiian Iced Tea (page 51).

SURLATABLE.COM
A great resource for infusion jars, glassware, knives, cutting boards, and many other bartending necessities.

THEMODERNMIXOLOGIST.COM
Tony Abou-Ganim, author of *Vodka Distilled* and *The Modern Mixologist*, sells a great line of bar tools on this site.

ZAMOURISPICES.COM
Sells cassia cinnamon bark and other spices and teas.

Index

Page numbers of photographs appear in italics.
Spirit types appear in bold.

About the Author

JULIE REINER has been elevating the cocktail scene in New York City for fifteen years, most notably with the opening of Flatiron Lounge (2003), Pegu Club (2005), Brooklyn's Clover Club (2008), and Lani Kai (2010). As co-owner and beverage director of Flatiron Lounge, Reiner drew much of her inspiration from her native Hawaii by utilizing the freshest fruits and premier-quality spices and spirits available in her original cocktails. Reiner's beverage program at Clover Club is highly focused on classics and furthers her signature style of superior quality and green-market ingredients. Lani Kai (recently sold), featured Pacific Rim plates and a more tropical interpretation of Reiner's cocktail styling. Her consulting company, Mixtress Consulting, helps create top-notch beverage programs and cocktails for restaurants, bars, resorts, and spirits companies.

Flatiron Lounge, Pegu Club, and Clover Club opened to rave reviews and have enjoyed top rankings among the best bars in the world. In 2009, Clover Club was honored with the award for Best New Cocktail Lounge in the World at Tales of the Cocktail. In 2013, it took home the awards for Best American Cocktail Bar and Best High Volume Bar, and Reiner was personally awarded Best Bar Mentor. Clover Club has also been listed in Drinks International's World's 50 Best Bars two years in a row.

Reiner's recipes have been featured in the *New York Times*, *New York* magazine, *Food & Wine*, *Imbibe*, the *Wall Street Journal*, *Esquire*, *Playboy*, *Gourmet*, *Food Arts*, *Bon Appétit*, *GQ*, *Fortune*, *Wine Enthusiast*, *O*, *Crain's New York Business*, *Time Out New York* and *Time Out London*, the London *Times*, and *Wine & Spirits*. Reiner has also been featured on the *Today* show, the Food Network, the Cooking Channel, Martha Stewart Radio, CNBC, LX.TV, and the Fine Living network. In 2011, Reiner was honored with a James Beard nomination for spirits professional of the year.